BIBLE LAND JOURNEY

including

Moments with Simon Peter

BIBLE LAND JOURNEY

including

Moments with Simon Peter

Dr. Johnny Loye King

ISBN 978-1-7386720-2-8

Johnny Loye King Publishing

Dedicated to

Judy Carol King

My wonderful wife and travelling companion for over 50 years.

Acknowledgments

I wish to thank:

My wife, Judy King, to whom this book is dedicated, for her invaluable help in layout and design.

Elisabeth Mullins who proofread the text and offered helpful suggestions.

Amy Doty, who travelled on the Premier Bible Land Journey in 2019 and is responsible for most of the photos including the cover.

Douglas and Maleah Walker, our pastor and friends, who have made our travels more enjoyable and informative.

Dr. Nathaniel Wilson, visionary, teacher, friend, for permission to include his moving writing entitled The Death of Moses.

All the ministers and families who have traveled to the Holy Land with me, some on multiple occasions, for all the thought provoking discussions we have had on the bus, at the sites, at the table, and walking together down the old paths.

Grace, Avi and Christiana for making every journey a joy.

Sincere and grateful thanks.
Johnny King

Contents

Contents, Cont.

Contents, Cont.

Welcome!

Bible Land Journey (Including Moments with Simon Peter) can be used in personal prayer and study or as a travel companion during your own Bible Land journey. The sites described here are not intended to be a comprehensive list of all biblical or historical sites in Israel (and possibly Jordan), nor are they exhaustively studied. These are the major sites visited during the Premier Bible Land Journey. It is designed specifically with ministers and students of the Bible in mind. On any given journey in the Bible Lands, numerous significant sites are driven past every day with little or no mention. This book will attempt to identify some of those places to increase your overall knowledge and appreciation of the land of the Bible.

Every journey to Israel, whether in person or through books like this, should visit the places where the scriptures place the Lord Jesus. This was, after all, where God chose to manifest himself in flesh and reveal himself to the world in the face of Jesus Christ. Special attention has also been given to the life and ministry of Simon Peter; the apostle given the keys to the kingdom of heaven by Jesus. Effort has been made to "put you in the moment and in the mind" of Simon Peter as he experienced the highs and lows of his life with Jesus.

Although this book may be prayerfully read anywhere, the ultimate enjoyment is to carry it with you in the land of the Bible. Read each section prior to visiting a particular site or, if possible, find a quiet place while you are at the site to read and reflect on what is written and what happened in this place. Scriptural references are provided to encourage you to read the passages in the Bible that pertain to events that happened at each site. Extra space has been included so that you can write down your thoughts and feelings. In years to come, this book will be a record of what you experienced as you visited places mentioned in your Bible. Write about what you saw, felt, and thought during your visit. Insert the date you visited each site.

In the back pages will be found a list of sites in alphabetical order, a scripture index, an explanation of the Bronze and Iron Ages and Historical Periods in the Levant, and Maps with the locations of the sites mentioned.

God bless you on your Bible Land Journey. May it be to you, as it has been to so many others, a spiritual experience that is both educational and inspirational.

Johnny Loye King

1

Lod לֹד (Lydda; *strife.* NT) and Ono אוֹנוֹ (*Strong, Vigorous*)

When you fly into Israel, you will land on a piece of ancient history. Ben Gurion airport (TLV) is situated between the Old Testament sites of Lod and Ono. The Ben Gurion airport was formerly known as the Lod airport and before that as the Lydda airport. Lydda and Lod are the same place. It was called Lod in the Old Testament and Lydda in the New Testament. It was at Lydda that the apostle Peter "found a certain man named Aeneas, which had kept his bed eight years…and said unto him, Aeneas, Jesus Christ maketh thee whole: arise, and make thy bed." And he arose immediately. And all that dwelt at Lydda and Saron saw him, and turned to the Lord (Acts 9:33, 34). While Peter was here at Lydda, two men came to him "desiring him that he would not delay to come" to Joppa where a woman named Tabitha had died (Acts 9:36-38). The modern city has reverted to using the Old Testament name of Lod.

Both Lod and Ono were mentioned as being developed by the tribe of Benjamin (1 Chron. 8:12) and were also the homes of over 700 exiles who returned from Babylon during the time of Ezra and Nehemiah (Ezra 2:33, Nehemiah 7:37, 11:35). Between 1950-1952, over 120,000 Jews who were descendants of those who remained in Babylon were brought back to Israel in Operation Ezra and Nehemiah. A Museum and Babylonian Jewry Heritage Center can be found in modern day Ono, also known as Or Yehuda. It is very possible that the airport is located on the very "plain of Ono" where Sanballat and Tobiah invited

Nehemiah to meet them "in one of the villages of the plain of Ono" when the wall of Jerusalem was being rebuilt (Nehemiah 6:1, 2). Nehemiah, suspecting a trap, replied, "Oh no! I am doing a great work and cannot come down." When the enemy of your soul invites you to a peace conference in the Valley of Ono, you should always reply, "Oh no!"

2

Joppa יָפוֹא and Ἰόππη (*Beautiful*) (Yafo, Yaffa, Jaffa) and Tel Aviv

Since 1950, the name of this city has officially been Tel Aviv-Yafo. "Tel Aviv" comes from the biblical site Telabib, where Ezekiel sat among "them of the captivity of Talabib" (Eze. 3:15). "Tel" means "mound" and we will visit many "tels" in Israel as we visit the sites of ancient settlements. "Abib" or "Aviv" means "spring." Tel Aviv has one of the highest costs of living of any city in the world. It is considered the "party capital" of the Middle East and is the Vegan Capital of the World with the most vegans per capita. Although it was only founded in 1909, Tel Aviv quickly outgrew the ancient town of Yafo, Yaffa, Joppa, and merged with it to become Tel Aviv-Yafo. When you go back home, visit your local supermarket and find Yaffa (or Jaffa) oranges in the fruit section. This is where they come from.

Yafo, or biblical Joppa, is one of the oldest human settlements in the world, and the Port of Joppa is a natural harbor that has been in use since the Bronze Age. The earliest known mention of

Joppa is in an ancient Egyptian letter from 1440 B.C. telling of the capture of Joppa by the Egyptian army when it was still a Canaanite city. It is mentioned again in the Amarna letters from 1360-1332 B.C. The Egyptians ruled here until around 800 B.C. Alexander the Great's troops were stationed here. The Crusaders captured the city from the Muslims during the First Crusade in 1099. Saladin captured it back in 1187 but it surrendered to Richard the Lionheart in 1191. The Egyptian Mamluks took Joppa in 1268 and it remained under Muslim rule, either Mamluk or Ottoman, until Napoleon captured it in 1799 and slew thousands of captured Muslim soldiers. This city has seen war and bloodshed for thousands of years.

This was the port where the cedars of Lebanon were floated before being transported to Jerusalem for Solomon's Temple (2 Chron. 2:16) and again to rebuild the Temple under Ezra (Ezra 3:7). Joppa was the base from which Old Testament Jonah and New Testament Peter were sent with a message of mercy to the Gentiles. It was at Joppa where Jonah boarded a ship bound for Tarshish (possibly Spain) to escape his call to Gentile ministry in Nineveh (Jonah 1:1-3), and it was here that Simon Peter stubbornly resisted God's command to eat of meats that were not allowed under Jewish Law (Acts 10:5-23).

It went something like this:

Simon Peter at Joppa

If there was anyone who should have been able to listen to the Lord, it was you. You had gone up on the housetop to pray. At about noon, while you were waiting for lunch to be prepared, you fell into a trance.[1] In the solitude of the housetop, while you waited, you were able to hear from the Lord. But having ears to hear, you heard not…at least not immediately.

To paraphrase, the Lord said, "Do this." You said, "No." The Lord said, "Don't argue with me." This sequence happened three times, one right after the other. You were hearing but you weren't quick to obey. After this amazing dialogue, you were left wondering what it was all about. You may even have doubted that it had really happened. About that time, though, strangers from Caesarea were knocking on the door and the Spirit spoke to you one more time, instructing you to go with these men and not to doubt. It took a while, but finally you were listening. You obeyed.

Peter's roof-top vision was God's way of preparing him for ministry to the Gentiles. It was here, at the house of Simon the tanner by the sea, that Cornelius had sent his servants at the angel's command to find Simon Peter who would come to Caesarea and "tell thee what thou oughtest to do." What happened here, in Joppa, had lasting significance for all Gentile Christians. As you walk the streets of ancient Joppa, listen for the voice of God. He may be telling you to witness to someone of a different ethnicity. And whatever you do, do not argue with God.

---

[1]This was probably a state of semi-consciousness somewhere between asleep and awake. It seems that it is easier to hear from God when our mind has ceased its own activity.

3

Caesarea by the Sea

Not to be confused with Caesarea Philippi, this Caesarea was the most important Roman city in all of Israel during the time of Jesus and the apostles. You won't find Caesarea in the Old Testament because it was built by Herod the Great around the same time that he was rebuilding the Temple in Jerusalem. The Romans called this Caesarea Maritima or Caesarea Palestinae. It was built near the site of a Phoenician naval station known as Strato's (Straton's) Tower. It was from here that Rome watched over the Empire's Provinces of Roman Judea, Syria Palaestina and Byzantine Palaestina. Herod named this city in honor of the Roman emperor, Caesar Augustus. An artificial harbor was built but did not survive because it used inferior and poorly mixed concrete which could not stand up to the seismic action that resulted from being built over a geologic fault line. Like Joppa, Caesarea changed hands many times because of various conquerors.

This is where Rabbi Abbahu lived, and Rabbi Akiva was executed. There was an extensive library here where Origen, Eusebius and Jerome studied. A new $25-million visitor centre recently opened to display some of the archeological findings of Caesarea within the period/modern reconstruction of four massive storage vaults built by Herod the Great.

Philip the Evangelist

After the great revival in Samaria where Philip baptized people "in the name of the Lord Jesus" (Acts 8:16) and watched them receive the Holy Ghost when Peter and John came down from Jerusalem, Philip was instructed by an angel to go to the desert between Jerusalem and Gaza. There he met the Ethiopian, "preached unto him Jesus," and "baptized him" (Acts 8:26-39). The importance and essentiality of baptism is emphasized when God would send an angel to instruct a preacher to travel many miles into the desert to preach to one man and immediately after baptizing him, "the Spirit of the Lord caught away Philip, that the eunuch saw him no more." "But Philip was found at Azotus (Ashdod): and passing through he preached in all the cities, till he came to Caesarea" (Acts 8:40). So, Philip wound up here after the revival in Samaria and after baptizing the Ethiopian eunuch. Apparently, Philip stayed here in Caesarea. Paul stayed in his house many days on his return from his third missionary journey.

> "And the next day we that were of Paul's company departed and came unto Caesarea: and we entered into the house of Philip the evangelist, which was one of the seven; and abode with him. And the same man had four daughters, virgins, which did prophesy. And we tarried there many days…" (Acts 21:8-10).

There are several items of particular interest to see in Caesarea.

The Pilate Stone – Before the discovery of this stone in 1961, some unlearned Bible sceptics argued that Pontius Pilate was not found in historic records as being a prefect for the Romans during the crucifixion of Jesus. But the ruins of Caesarea were not excavated until the 1950s and 1960s. The stone was discovered holding up a stairway behind the stage of the theatre. It had been reused like many other ancient stones have been throughout the centuries. It is authentic and from the 1st century. The Latin reads:

[DIS AUGUSTI]S TIBERIEUM
[..........PONTI]US PILATUS
[..........PRAEF]ECTUS JUDA[EA]E
[....FECIT D]E[DICAVIT]

Translated into English, it would read:
"To the Divine Augustus [this] Tiberium...Pontius Pilate... prefect of Judea...has dedicated [this]"

The original stone is in the Israel Museum in Jerusalem. The replica stands in the ruins of Herod's palace, which later became Pilate's palace. As you look at the inscription, be confident that the Bible is true regardless of what the sceptics say. (To this point, no sceptics have apologized for their false claim that Pontius Pilate did not serve as mentioned in the Gospels.)

Pilate Stone—Photo Credit Amy Doty

The Theatre: Herod Agrippa – The ancient theatre, like the rest of Caesarea, was covered by sand dunes. The sand helped preserve the remains of this Roman style theatre. It has a seating capacity of 3,500. In Roman Empire days, it could be covered by massive tarps giving shade to those sitting on the stone benches. Some of the benches have been replaced and some are original. The theatre is still used for concerts today. The stage had a high backdrop that was used during theatrical and musical productions. It totally blocked the view of the ocean that the audience would otherwise have seen. The ocean view would have been a distraction. The backdrop also helped the acoustics by projecting sound out toward the audience and blocking the sound of wind and waves from the ocean. There are still grooves in the stones of the two passageways leading from the floor of the theatre on either end of the stage. Stone or wooden gates were placed in these grooves, allowing the floor to be flooded with water so that theatrical water scenes and naval battles could be acted out.

Acts 12 tells how Herod Agrippa I killed James with the sword. After he saw that this "pleased the Jews," he proceeded to imprison Peter. But when Peter was led out of the prison by the angel, Herod put the jailers to death and left Jerusalem for Caesarea. "On a set day Herod, arrayed in royal apparel, sat upon his throne, and made an oration unto" the people in Caesarea. This theatre was probably where Herod Agrippa addressed the crowd. And it also appears that he died here immediately following his speech in A.D. 44 "because he gave not God the glory." (Another possible location of this speech would have been the hippodrome.)

The Palace of Herod the Great: Paul – Originally built as Herod's seaside palace, it became the official residence of the Roman prefect, procurator, or governor. Thus, during the crucifixion, this was the home of Pontius Pilate. He would have travelled to Jerusalem during the major feast days as the representative of the emperor. Later, it served as the headquarters for Felix and then Porcius Festus. It is most likely that the Apostle Paul was kept in one of the numerous rooms here for two years after he had been accused by the Jews. It was here that he preached to Felix, and Felix (who was married to a Jewess) "trembled, and answered, 'Go thy way for this time; when I have a convenient season, I will call for thee.'" Festus succeeded Felix in office and tried Paul again. Attempting to please the Jews, Festus asked Paul to go to be tried at Jerusalem. Paul finally realized he would not receive a fair trial. The Jews were determined to kill him. This is when Paul appealed to Caesar, his right as a Roman citizen. Then King Agrippa II arrived in Caesarea with his sister Bernice for a visit with Festus. Probably this was to welcome Festus as procurator and make introductions. Festus, having Paul near at hand, explained the situation to King Agrippa who desired to hear Paul for himself. It was arranged the very next day. While Festus reacted by saying, "Paul, thou art beside thyself; much learning doth make thee mad," Agrippa said, "Almost thou persuadest me to be a Christian." Perhaps his father's death in such a horrible fashion, not much more than a stone's throw from where he now sat, had a sobering effect on him. He had only been a boy of seventeen years when that had happened and was probably present in Caesarea at the time. But now, this King of Batanaea, Trachonitis, Gaulanitis, Tiberias, Taricheae and Peraean Julias had come seemingly face to face with the God who had slain his father. He was almost persuaded but there is no record that he ever accepted the Gospel. He was the last Herod, dying at the age of 73, in the third year of Emperor Trajan. (It was suggested by both Josephus and Juvenal that Agrippa and Bernice lived together incestuously, although Bernice had an affair with Titus during the First Jewish War that ended after Titus became emperor.)

After two years in this location, preaching to Roman governors and a king and his sister, Paul sailed from this harbor on his way to appear before Caesar. It was to be his last missionary journey.

Remains of Herod's Palace at Caesarea by the Sea
Photo Credit Amy Doty

The Hippodrome – From two Greek words, *hippos* meaning horse and *dromos* meaning course, a *hippodrome* was a stadium for horse and chariot racing. The Romans called it a circus. It was here that gladiatorial contests also took place. And it was here that

2,500 Jews were killed in 70 A.D. following the Jewish revolt. (Although it is more likely that Herod Agrippa gave his last speech in the theatre, the hippodrome is another possible location.)

Peter and Cornelius: The Gentile Connection – Of greatest importance to us, Caesarea was the site of the Gospel being preached to the Gentiles, and those Gentiles receiving the gift of the Holy Ghost and speaking with tongues. Peter then commanded them to be baptized in the name of the Lord Jesus (Acts 10).

As you wander these grounds, remember that there was an honest soldier, Cornelius, a centurion of the Italian band, who was sincerely seeking to please God. He lived in this city. An angel of the Lord appeared to him here in this place and instructed him to send for Simon Peter. Think of Peter on the housetop in Joppa, a few miles south, arguing with God about what he would and would not eat. Imagine Peter coming to this place and preaching to the Gentiles for the very first time. Listen for voices on the wind. If you have received the Holy Ghost, the same Spirit that fell upon you, causing you to speak with tongues, fell first upon Gentiles in this place. That same Spirit is present in this place to this day. Lift your eyes to the heavens and thank God for the angel, the preacher, the household of Cornelius, and the promise of the Holy Ghost that fell in this place. Remember that the people who received the Holy Ghost in this place were commanded (strong words) to be baptized in the name of the Lord Jesus and let your faith in the apostolic message be strengthened.

4

Roman Aqueduct

Caesarea had no fresh water to support it, so Herod had a Roman style aqueduct built to carry water from the Carmel mountains nearly ten miles away. Using a series of arches, and precise engineering, the structure supplied fresh water to the capital. Later, Emperor Hadrian had an additional channel added to increase the capacity. Much of the aqueduct still stands, a proud testimony of Roman engineering, and of the building projects that made Herod "the Great."

The apostle Paul doubtless drank of the water that flowed through this aqueduct, as did Peter, Cornelius, Philip and numerous other biblical and historical figures. But the aqueduct failed centuries ago. This marvel of engineering has fallen into disrepair. The water no longer flows. The best of man's plans and building expertise could not keep the waters flowing. But the Holy Ghost that was poured out in Caesarea, where this aqueduct led, has ever been flowing. The "rivers of living water" promised by Jesus are still flowing (John 7:37). Have you tasted this water? "The promise is unto you, and to your children, and to all that are afar off…" (Acts 2:38-39).

Roman Aqueduct—Photo Credit Amy Doty

5

Mt. Carmel כַּרְמֶל (*Fruitful, Plentiful field or place*)

Mount Carmel, or "Carmel by the sea" (Jer. 46:18), is most famous for the prophets Elijah and Elisha. The entire mountain range is referred to as "Mount Carmel," but the area located at the northwestern tip of the range is where Elijah challenged the prophets of Baal (1 Kings 18:17-40). It was here, near Jezreel and above the brook Kishon, that Elijah told King Ahab to assemble all Israel, 450 prophets of Baal and 400 of the prophets of the groves that ate at Jezebel's table.

Elijah said, "the God that answereth by fire, let him be God." The prophets of Baal offered their sacrifice and called on the name of Baal from morning until noon and on until the time of the evening sacrifice, probably about 3:00 pm. Their worship service lasted between 6 and 9 hours. Their effort was wasted. There was no voice, no answer, nor any that regarded.

Elijah said to the people, "Come near." He repaired the altar of the LORD that was broken down, dug a trench around it, put wood and a bullock on the altar and saturated it with 12 barrels of water. Then he prayed a 30-second prayer and the fire of the LORD fell and consumed the burnt sacrifice, the wood, the stones, the dust and the water that was in the trench.

When the people saw it, they fell on their faces and said, "The LORD, he is the God; the LORD, he is the God."

Elijah said, "Take the prophets of Baal; let not one escape." Then he took them down to the foot of the mountain on the north side, to the brook Kishon (visible from the lookout on top of Carmel) and slew them there.

He told Ahab, "The drought is almost over. There is a sound of abundance of rain." Then he climbed up to the top of the mountain again. Now he prayed longer than 30-seconds.

James 5:16-18 "The effectual fervent prayer of a righteous man availeth much. Elias was a man subject to like passions as we are, and he prayed earnestly that it might not rain: and it rained not on the earth by the space of three years and six months. And he prayed again, and the heaven gave rain, and the earth brought forth her fruit."

From our viewpoint we know we are near the place, perhaps on the very spot, where this story took place. Looking one direction, you can see the Mediterranean and in the other direction you can see the brook Kishon.

Cloud like a man's hand 1 Kings 18:41-44
Race to Jezreel and the rain 1 Kings 18:45-46
Elisha and the woman of Shunem 2 Kings 4:25

(Note: The Carmel mentioned in the story of David and Abigail is not Mount Carmel. It is a place in Judah, close to Hebron where David was hiding from Saul. 1 Sam. 25.)

View from Mt. Carmel—Valley of Armageddon
Photo Credit Amy Doty

6

Tel Megiddo מְגִדּוֹ (*Rendezvous or Place of Crowds*) and Valley of Armageddon

Also known as Tel al-Mutesellim (Arabic), lit. "Mound of the Governor," and Har Megiddo which means "Mount of Megiddo" from which the name Armageddon derives. Archeological excavations have uncovered twenty-six different levels of occupation, dating from at least 3500 B.C. and many say 5000 B.C. Megiddo has the four criteria needed for occupation: strategic location, roads, agriculture and water. It was significant for its location controlling travel and trade along the Jezreel Valley (also known as the Valley of Armageddon) through which the most important trade route of the ancient world passed. More than 2,000 years before there was a Rome or a Roman Road, it might be said that all roads led past Megiddo. All goods and persons passing between Egypt and Mesopotamia and Asia Minor had to pass Megiddo as it guards the famous Via Maris. "Via Maris" is the LXX translation of Isaiah's (9:1) "the way of the sea." The Grand Trunk Road, also known as the International North-South Route, running north to south through Megiddo connected Egypt with Damascus.

Wars and Rumors of Wars

Because of its strategic location, about 34 battles were fought in this area, including several memorable battles. The first battle ever recorded, outside of the Bible, was when Thutmose III brought his Egyptian army here in 1479 B.C. and captured Megiddo from the Canaanites who had rebelled against Egyptian rule upon his accession to the throne. The account, inscribed on the walls of the Temple of Amun in Karnak, Egypt, says that he marched his men from Egypt to Yehem (near present day Ein Iron by the interchange of Hwys 6 and 65, 6 or 7 miles east of Caesarea) in ten days. There he stopped for a council with his generals to decide from which direction to attack Megiddo. There were three possibilities: a northern route which arrived at the Valley of Jezreel at Yokneam; a southern route which came out near Ta'anach; and a route right through the center that came out at Megiddo. His generals recommended he take the northern or southern route because they were more open, easier to pass through and to defend from ambush. Thutmose reasoned that this is what the Canaanites would be counting on. They wouldn't believe that he was dumb enough to take the central route which was narrower and where his army could be easily ambushed. Therefore, he did what was least expected and hoped he could catch the Canaanites by surprise. It took him twelve hours to march his army though the pass, known variously as the Nahal Iron (Iron River), Wadi Ara or the Musmus Pass. As Thutmose expected, the Canaanites were guarding the other two passes and were thus surprised and defeated. Unfortunately for Thutmose, in the time it took for his men to defeat the two enemy camps and plunder their goods, the few old men, boys and women left in Megiddo were able to close the city gates, resulting in a siege that lasted seven months before the Egyptians could capture the city. This difficulty in taking a walled city might explain why some of the cities remained standing after Joshua's conquest of the land.

From your vantage point on top of Megiddo, you can see where Deborah and Barak's ten thousand men chased Jabin's 900 chariots under Sisera from Mt. Tabor to the Kishon river (Judges 4).

To the south Gideon's three companies surrounded the thousands of Midianites in the valley between Gideon's spring and Mt. Moreh, and Saul travelled through the night to visit the witch at Endor and died the next day at Gilboa. Megiddo witnessed it all.

In WWI, General Edmund Allenby, a student of history who had read a translation of Thutmose III's account, used the same tactics to bring about a victory over German and Turkish forces thus winning another Battle of Megiddo in September 1918 and capturing hundreds of enemy soldiers without the loss of one man. In between these two battles, Megiddo witnessed many famous armies and commanders marching past, including Alexander the Great and the Roman General Titus. There were four separate battles between Saladin and the Crusaders in the 12th century. The Mamluks from Egypt defeated the Mongols near Harod Spring in 1260, stopping the Mongol advance. In 1799, Napoleon with an army of 4,000 defeated an Ottoman army of 35,000 near Mt. Tabor. The Turks fled toward the mountains to the south and to the Jordan. Napoleon reportedly said, "All the armies in the world could maneuver their forces on this vast plain… There is no place in the whole world more suited for war than this… It is the most natural battleground of the whole earth." [2]

---

[2] Cline, Eric H., The Battles of Armageddon: Megiddo and the Jezreel Valley from the Bronze Age to the Nuclear Age (Ann Arbor, MI: University of Michigan, 2002), 142.

Tribe of Manasseh

Joshua defeated 31 kings on the west side of Jordan, including the kings of Jokneam, Megiddo and Ta'anach (Jos 12:7-24). Megiddo was in territory that was allotted to the tribe of Manasseh but according to Joshua 17:11-13, they could not drive out the inhabitants but eventually put them to tribute (Judges 1:27, 28).

This ridge of hills and mountains at the southern border of the Jezreel Valley formed the northern border of the half tribe of Manasseh.

Josiah

The last revival before Babylonian captivity was during the reign of Josiah, the son of Manasseh. Josiah began to reign when he was eight years old. "He did that which was right in the sight of the LORD, and walked in all the ways of David his father, and turned not aside to the right hand or to the left" (2 Kings 22:2). Josiah was one of the best kings Judah ever saw. When he was eighteen, he cleaned out and repaired the temple in Jerusalem, where they rediscovered the law of God. He defiled the high places, destroyed the images and tore down altars to false gods throughout Judah and Samaria. When he was 26 years old, he held a Passover like none other "from the days of the judges that judged Israel, nor in all the days of the kings of Israel, nor of the kings of Judah" (2 Kings 23:22). Unfortunately for Judah, all of Josiah's reforms were too late. Judgment was held off only as long as Josiah lived. When Pharoah-Neco came through this valley to fight the king of Assyria, "king Josiah went against him; and he (Pharoah) slew him (Josiah) at Megiddo" (2 Kings 23:29). So, it was here that this young king, one of the best Judah ever had, was slain in battle.

Discoveries at Megiddo

Megiddo was completely covered by the winds of time. The centuries of dust and leaves on the site thoroughly disguised the location. Though the American minister Edward Robinson made some stunning discoveries when he travelled through the land in 1838 (think Robinson's Arch), Megiddo was one of his most spectacular mistakes. He was actually here, standing over Megiddo. Of this hill, he said, "This would indeed present a splendid site for a city; but there is no trace, of any kind, to show that a city ever stood here." The identity of Megiddo was made by 1896 and the first excavations began in 1903. It is currently in its fourth excavation and yet only about one quarter of the site has been uncovered.

Six-Chamber Gate

Enter the site through the Canaanite gateway. An inner gate consists of the remaining three chambers of a six-chamber gate that was probably built by Solomon. 1 Kings 9:15 reveals that Solomon built the walls of "Hazor, and Megiddo, and Gezer." These gates were advanced technology for city defense. If an enemy were able to breach the outer wall, there were soldiers within and upon the chambers of the gate from which to fire upon the enemy. In time of peace, the chambers could be used to billet soldiers or store weapons. The center chamber of this gate has been filled in with stones.

Gate-Tel Megiddo—Photo Credit Amy Doty

Grain Silo

Traveling through the prairies of the US and Canada, one can see grain silos rising about the railroad tracks of every small town. In the ancient middle east, most storage silos were dug into the ground and lined with stones. This silo was built in the 8th century B.C. during the reign of King Jeroboam. It has a capacity of 450 cubic meters. Two sets of stairways are set into the walls allowing people to ascend and descend. Silos like this were built in Egypt by Joseph to store the grain from the bountiful seven years before the famine.

Water Tunnel

Thought to date from the reign of King Ahab, who lived just down the street in Jezreel, a shaft 115 feet deep was sunk, and a tunnel dug to connect with the spring that was just outside the city walls. To provide for the city and to deprive the enemy of water in case of siege, the spring was walled up and camouflaged with the only access from within the walls. The tunnel is about 330 feet in length. Workmen began at both ends and dug toward the middle. When they met, they were only about 12 inches off center, quite an accomplishment for that time. This is very similar to Hezekiah's tunnel in Jerusalem which was dug for the same reason.

Solomon's Stables

These long buildings are believed to be stables for Solomon's (some say Ahab's) horses. There is a school of thought that these were for grain storage similar to those found atop Masada, but the later construction of the grain pit as well as the discovery of stone mangers for feeding and watering animals lend credence to them being stables. Note that the mangers are made of stone, as were most mangers in the Bible Land. The Christmas picture of baby Jesus laying in a manger made of wood is most likely false. Jesus would probably have lain in a manger like these, padded with clean straw and articles of clothing.

The Great Temple

This 5,000-year-old temple is the largest edifice discovered in the Levant from the Early Bronze Age. Measuring 155 by 75 feet, it ranks among the largest structures of its time and is more than ten times larger than the normal temple of that time period.

Round Altar

A prominent circular stone structure is thought to be a Canaanite altar or a high place. Pastor Ken Bow worked here for a season on a biannual excavation team. After discovering some small animal bones that excited the team leaders, Pastor Bow said they were Kentucky Fried Chicken. In other words, they were nothing more than lunch remains for ancient workers. The professional archeologists mocked him and said they were no doubt part of animal sacrifices. After flying specialists in from far away, the project manager came up to him and said, "You were right. Kentucky Fried Chicken."

Megiddo Church

Near Megiddo, at the site of the Megiddo Prison, excavations in 2005 discovered a mosaic with the words, "The God loving Akeptous has offered the table to God Jesus Christ as a memorial," dating from 230 A.D. Before this discovery, critics said that Jesus was not worshipped as God until the Council of Nicaea in 325 A.D. This discovery silences that particular criticism as it predates Nicaea by 100 years. Another inscription names a Roman centurion as "Gaianus" who was also called "Porophrius, our brother." This reveals that almost a century before Christianity was legalized in the Roman Empire, there were places where it flourished even under Roman officials. Of course, Cornelius may have had some influence upon the liberty of Christians in Caesarea even during the time of the Apostles. This appears to be the world's oldest "purpose built" church, bumping the Aqaba Church (c. 293-303) to second place. The prison complex (until it is demolished to make way for a planned visitor's center) is visible from the top of Tel Megiddo by looking SSE. It is on the southeast corner of the intersection of Highways 65 and 66.

7

Gideon's Spring (Ein Harod)

Gideon (Judges 7)

Coming out of the foot of Mount Gilboa, and near Jezreel, is the spring called in Judges 7:1, "the well of Harod." The small valley here is a watershed. Whereas the Jezreel Valley drains west into the Mediterranean Sea, the Harod Valley drains east into the Jordan River and thus into the Dead Sea. It was here that Gideon's 32,000 camped, across the narrow valley from Mt. Moreh, directly north, which protected the rear of the Midianite army. After 22,000 of Gideon's men were allowed to leave, God tested the remaining 10,000 by having them drink at these waters. The 300 men that were left, divided into three companies, and that night, with their trumpets, pitchers and lamps, surrounded the Midianite camp. I imagine them positioning one company west of the Midianites, one company southwest and the other company south. When the trumpets sounded, the pitchers were broken and the lamps were exposed. Three hundred men, each of them a captain, shouted the charge, "The sword of the LORD, and of Gideon!" The Midianites broke and ran, cutting one another down in their confusion. The survivors ran east down the Valley of Harod, past Bethshean and to the Jordan, where the men of Ephraim captured and killed the two princes of the Midianites.

Gideon Springs—Photo Credit Amy Doty

King Saul (1 Sam 28 & 31)

About 180 years after Gideon's great victory over the Midianites, the armies of Israel and its enemies were encamped in the same locations. This time, the enemy was the Philistines, camped at Shunem with their back to Mount Moreh, and Israel, on Mount Gilboa, was led by King Saul. Saul, having silenced the voice of the man of God even before Samuel had died, was desperate to hear from God. He travelled from Mount Gilboa under the cover of darkness, to Endor (Ein Dor), to the northeast of Mt. Moreh to consult with a witch.

In a strange and difficult to understand account, the witch brought up Samuel from the dead, who prophesied to Saul that he and his sons would be killed the next day. Saul ate the meal of the condemned at the witch's house in Endor before traveling back to Gilboa, arriving just in time to go into battle. The king had not slept all night. He fought under a curse. He died in Mount Gilboa. His armor was displayed in the temple of Ashtoreth and the bodies of Saul, and his sons were hung on the wall of Bethshean.

8

Sea of Galilee גָּלִיל and Γαλιλαία (*Circuit* or *The Heathen Circle*)

Also known as Gennesaret, Ginosar, Kinneret, Kinnoreth and Lake Tiberias, the Sea of Galilee is the lowest freshwater lake on earth with a surface that varies between 686-705 feet below sea level. It is 33 miles around, 13 miles long by 8 miles wide with a maximum depth of 141 feet. Bethsaida and Capernaum were fishing towns on the lake during the time of Jesus. Much of His ministry took place surrounding this lake with some events taking place on the lake itself. Ernest Renan said the Galilean landscape was the Fifth Gospel. The song that says, "Let's all go down to the river, there's a man walking on the water," is not biblical. But Jesus walking on the water here on the Sea of Galilee is biblical. Intense storms arise suddenly as strong winds blow over the water from the east, coming down from the Golan Heights to stir up violent waves that have washed up into the streets of Tiberius. It was such a storm that caught the disciples by surprise and almost capsized their boat when Jesus came to them walking on the water.

Ancient Galilee Boat

Josephus said there were 230 fishing boats regularly fishing the lake in the first century. One of the boats from that era was found preserved in the mud near the shore of Kibbutz Ginnosar in 1986. They excavated the boat without damaging it; treated it to protect it, and now display it in the Yigal Alon museum on the kibbutz. It measures 27 feet long by 7.5 feet wide and is an example of the boats that would have been used by Jesus and His disciples. It just could be one of the same boats.

We board a larger and more modern boat to sail from one point to another on the lake. Whether it happens in daytime or at night, a voyage on the Sea of Galilee is always a special and memorable experience. Imagine Jesus on these same waters, on a calm day or a stormy night. Here, that dark and stormy night, Peter said, "Lord, if it be thou, bid me come to thee walking on the water. And He said, 'Come'" (Matt 14:22-33).

Ancient Galilee Boat—Photo Credit Amy Doty

Simon Peter at Galilee - Scene one (Luke 5:1-11)

It's a calm morning. You've been fishing all night and have caught nothing. Not even a nibble. Every cast has come back empty. Your muscles ache from drawing the net back into the boat time after fruitless time. There is nothing between your belly button and your backbone except hunger. At least the long night is over. You've brought the boat to shore and spread out your nets to dry and fold. The job is almost done, and you look forward to going home where you know there will be fresh bread, still warm from the oven. You will stretch and rest from the night of work. You hear a hubbub and glance up. A crowd is approaching. Jesus is in the front. He nods at you as He strides past and climbs into your boat. The crowd keeps coming. You have to grab the last of your nets to keep them from being trod upon and tangled. Jesus sits down in the boat and begins to teach the people. You sigh. How long will this last? At least, He's a good teacher. You are soon spellbound. You forget your tiredness and your hunger.

All too soon, He is finished. He looks directly at you. His look makes you nervous. It feels as if He can see into the depths of your soul. It's like He knows your every thought. Suddenly you're a child caught snatching sweets from your mother's oven. You think, "What now?" He says, "Take me out into the deep and let down your nets for a big catch." Your stomach growls loud enough for Him to hear. He smiles. You look at your neatly folded nets. "Master, we've fished all night and caught nothing. They're not running. They've gone to the bottom. It will be a waste of time." "And…" you think, but don't say, "…and a waste of energy. And I'm so tired and hungry." He tilts His head and raises one eyebrow. You hear yourself saying, "I wouldn't do this for anyone else, but because it's You…" Andrew looks at you like you're crazy. He starts to say something but thinks better of it when you glare at him and start throwing nets back into the boat.

Jesus sits staring across the lake as you work your stiff muscles getting the boat back out into deep water. Finally, you prepare to throw the net over the side. Jesus has transferred His gaze from the far shore to your face and is watching you with keen interest. The net goes out. It barely settles under the water when it begins to pull and tug. What's this? Your mind can't comprehend what's happening. You shout at Andrew and he jumps to help you pull in the net. Both of you together can't bring it in. Your excited yells have caught the attention of James and John. You gesture to them and they maneuver their boat to help you draw up the net. Muscles strain. Your breath comes in short gasps, gasps of wonder as well as shortness of breath from the exertion. When the net is in, both boats have been filled beyond reasonable capacity. They sit so low in the water from the weight of fish that water comes in over the side. You will have to carefully work your way to shore to keep from sinking. The magnitude of what has just happened begins to dawn on you. You look up from the hundreds of squirming, flopping fish. Jesus is still examining you. You fall down before Him as He sits in your boat. You have forgotten your tiredness. You have forgotten your hunger. You pay no mind to the miraculous multitude of fish surrounding you. You forget James and John in the other boat. You forget your brother in your boat. The only muscle that you're aware of is your heart. It explodes. "Go away from me, Oh Lord, I'm a sinful man." His look says, "I know what you are, but I still love you." His voice says, "Don't worry. From now on you will catch men." We followed Him. All of us.

Simon Peter at Galilee - Scene two (Matthew 14:22-32)

In the storm, in the dark, you fear that your boat will capsize, and you will perish in the dark waters. Jesus sent you here. He said, "Get in a boat and go to the other side while I disperse this crowd." Night has fallen. The wind has come up and grown stronger. It's one of those sudden storms that the Galilee is known for. You've stopped making any headway toward Bethsaida, and are only trying to keep your bow headed into the wind so the waves don't tip you. A quick trip has turned into a night long struggle for survival. Everyone is hoping for the dawn and a calm, but it's only about three or four in the morning and there's not much hope you can hold out. Above the roar of the wind and the shouts of your comrades, one of their voices--a voice suddenly more fearful--penetrates your consciousness. A figure is seen approaching the boat. It looks like a spirit walking toward you. Is this the angel of death? Is this how you will die? Will it all end here on the sea? Fear of the storm mixes with fear of the unknown. Other voices are raised in fear. But the strange figure lifts His voice above the storm. "Courage! Don't be afraid. It's me." Jesus! In your fear, you see Him coming toward your boat. Can you believe it's Him? And after He identifies Himself, is your desire to go to Him stronger than your desire to remain safe in the boat? Dare you ask Him to invite you to do what no other man has ever done? Can you say it? "Lord, if it's really You, bid me come to You on the water." You wait. You are drenched. The storm still rages. Water sloshes around in the boat. The others have stopped bailing. Everyone is holding to the rail, the sail, the mast. Holding anything to keep from being thrown overboard. Unbelief mixes with fear. Are they hearing right? Did you just ask to walk on water? The wait was not long. All these questions and feelings happened in milliseconds. Jesus said, "Come on." Now what?

Simon Peter at Galilee - Scene three (John 21:3-22)

It's not the same. It's too quiet. It's just like it was back in Jerusalem. Everybody is sad. They're just lost. They don't know what to do when Jesus isn't around. When you announced, "I'm going fishing," six of the others stood up and said, "We're going with you." Now, here you are after a whole night on the water and nothing to show for it. The boat is not far from land, about a hundred yards. In the breaking light you see a figure on the shore. He says, "Boys, have you caught anything to eat?" You bristle at the term "Boys." It's a word only a person familiar with you would use, and then only when he might be implying that you were being a little immature or acting like children. Who does he think he is? One of the others says, "No." Then the man says, "Cast the net on the right side of the ship, and you will find." Almost without thinking, they cast the net on the right side, as though there would be more fish on one side of an eight-foot-wide boat than on the other. But before your thought can be completed, the boat leans toward the right side as though a heavy weight has filled the net. It's full of fish! Your mind is trying to process all the data it has received in the last couple of minutes. A feeling of "I've been here before" is nagging at you. This is when John leans toward you and says, "Peter, it is the Lord." Suddenly realization dawns. Without thinking, you shrug into your wrap and throw yourself into the water. As you make your way toward the shore you hear a babble of excitement behind you. The others, so quiet just moments before, are shouting and laughing as they wrestle with a huge haul of fish. You wade through the shallow water and come to Jesus. He's tending some fish on a bed of coals. He glances up at you, smiles, and says, "Go help the others bring in the fish." Relieved at being given a task by the One you call Master, you turn around and go help drag the net to land. Everyone helps count. A hundred-fifty-three fish. Jesus says, "Come and eat." Jesus passes out bread and fish.

After breakfast, Jesus turns to you and asks, "Simon, do you love me more than these?" Your mind is a whirl of emotions and questions. "These? These other men? What are You asking? Do I love You more than these men love you? Or do I love You more than I love them? These fish? This lifestyle? This occupation of fishing? These things? Boats? Nets?" You play it safe and say, "Lord, You know I love You." You've avoided the question, and you've done it rather poorly, answering "*phileo*" when He asked you "*agapao*." "Feed my lambs," Jesus says.

He does not pull you aside. The conversation is more painful because it is in full view of the others. It's like He is saying, "Peter, I'm gone a few days and you revert to your former life. This is what you were doing when I found you. What will you do after I leave? Will you follow me? Will you be what I called you to be? A fisher of men? Or will you spend the rest of your life on this lake struggling to make a living? Will your greatest joy be a good catch of fish?" All eyes were on Him. He could have been talking to all of them.

The second time Jesus says, "That's not what I asked you, Simon. Do you love (*agapao*) me?" Now the Master is not asking how much, or in comparison with something else. He asks if what you just said is true. "Do you love me?" You blush, remembering your denial, three denials, a few days ago. Your heart sinks within you. You don't even look up as you mutter, "Yes, Lord, You know I love (*phileo*) you." Jesus sighs, "Feed my sheep."

The third time He says, "Simon, do you love (*phileo*) me?" Three times you claimed you didn't know Him. And now, three times He wants you to affirm that you do. And that you don't just know Him, but that you love Him. Your heart, so light a little while ago when you found out Jesus was here, has become heavy. You are grieved, and answer, "Lord, You know everything. You know my frame. You know my failure. And You know that from the depths of my soul I love You." He says, "Feed my sheep. Truly, Peter, when you were young, you went where you wanted and did what you wanted. You liked the things of the flesh. But when you are old, you will stretch out your hands and someone else will carry you where you would not choose to go." That was crucifixion language. You shuddered, turned around and spotted John. "Lord, what about him?" "Don't worry about him. You follow me." You did. You followed Him to the end.

9

Capernaum Καπερναούμ (*Village of Comfort*)

This ancient fishing town on the northwest shore of the Sea of Galilee was Jesus' adopted hometown. "And leaving Nazareth, he came and dwelt in Capernaum" (Matt 4:13). Capernaum lies on the Via Maris (Way of the Sea – the major trade route between Syria and Egypt) as seen in the 2nd century Roman milestone found here, "That it might be fulfilled which was spoken by Esaias the prophet, saying, The land of Zabulon, and the land of Nephthalim, by the way of the sea" (Matt 4:14, 15). This might explain how "his fame went throughout all Syria" (Matt 4:24). It was here that He called the brothers Peter and Andrew while they were practicing the occupation of fishermen. He challenged them with, "Follow me, and I will make you fishers of men. And they straightway left their nets, and followed Him. And going on from thence, He saw other two brethren, James the son of Zebedee, and John his brother, in a ship with Zebedee their father, mending their nets; and he called them. And they immediately left the ship and their father, and followed Him" (Matt 4:19-22, Mark 1:1-37, Matt 8:5 – 9:34).

At least five of the apostles were chosen here: Peter and Andrew (fishermen, brothers), John and James (fishermen, brothers, sons of Zebedee), and Matthew (Levi, son of Alpheus, tax collector). The presence of a resident tax collector and a Roman centurion attest to this being an important town in the first century. It probably had a population of over 1,500 which was significant for that time and for this area.

The Franciscans purchased 2/3 of the area in 1894. The other third, to the east, is owned by the Greek Orthodox. The entire area of the village is 15 acres. Only about one-third of the whole area has been excavated. After Charles Warren uncovered the foundations of the synagogue, locals dug into the ground around the synagogue and the church to find limestone blocks to reuse as building materials and to burn for lime. This place became a quarry that was only protected because it was purchased by the Franciscans.

Numerous stone jetties confirm the importance of fishing and even shipping from other points to this port on the Roman road, which was built over the Way-of-the-Sea, connecting Damascus and Egypt and all points in between. Some of these jetties, on the eastern side of the village, become visible when the water level is very low. They extend about 100 feet into the lake, with some of them being curved inward toward one another, others jutting straight out and some being triangular in shape.

Synagogue

The white synagogue dates from the Late Roman period, toward the end of the 4th century. The white stones were found in the ruins, allowing for the reconstruction of what can be seen today. Other stones from the synagogue are still scattered around the site, including one with a carving of the ark of the covenant mounted on a cart. Black basalt stones are visible under the white stones on the western wall. This is the first century synagogue where Jesus would have taught and performed miracles. "And they went into Capernaum; and straightway on the Sabbath day he entered into the synagogue, and taught. And they were astonished at his doctrine: for he taught them as one that had authority, and not as the scribes" (Mark 1:21, 22). Synagogues were commonly built atop earlier synagogues for several practical reasons. The ground was already owned by the community. The site was already considered holy. It was easier to build upon a foundation already laid. Often, they reused some of the same stones. In this case, they rebuilt with white limestone imported from the Galilean hills west of the town instead of the more common local black basalt stones. (Basalt is a result of volcanic activity. There is no basalt south of the Jezreel Valley except for a tiny scattering in the Iskander Uplift southwest of Ta'anach.) Stone benches can be seen on the long walls. The columns arranged in lines at the front and sides of the main prayer hall held the roof and a balcony which may have been reserved for women. A door through the east wall leads to a courtyard, probably used as a fellowship hall. The typical 1st century synagogue in this area would have had stone benches around three sides, perhaps with two to four stepped tiers. Inside and to the right of the entrance was the Seat of Moses, a stone seat where the teacher would sit. A wooden reading lectern was placed on a decorated stone base and situated in the center of the hall. This is where the reader would stand and read from the Torah scroll.

In this synagogue:

- Jesus taught as one having authority, and not as the scribes (Mark 1:21, 22)
- Jesus delivered the man with the unclean spirit (Mark 1:23-26)
- The man with the withered hand (Mark 3:1-5)
- Jairus was a leader in this synagogue (Mark 5:22)

Dr Johnny King—Synagogue at Capernaum
Photo Credit Amy Doty

Ancient Street

Beside the black foundation stones of the synagogue are other black stones laid for a street that ran alongside the synagogue. Jesus and the apostles would have walked on these stones. This was street level in Jesus' day.

Simon Peter's House

This is where Simon and Andrew lived with their families. Simon's mother-in-law was healed by Jesus and immediately began feeding the disciples. The whole town gathered before the door of this house and Jesus healed many (Mark 1:29-34). On another day, the crowd was so great about the door that four men carried the palsied man on top of the house and uncovered the roof to let him down to where Jesus was teaching (Mark 2:1-12). An octagonal shaped Byzantine church was on this location. Excavations revealed that it had been built upon the ruins of a home that was inhabited in the first century. The first century house consisted of about ten rooms, most of which were arranged around an inner courtyard. It was probably one of these rooms that Jesus slept in while in Capernaum. Another sizable courtyard bordered the harbor and was probably where work was done such as cleaning and folding nets, and for the drying and selling of fish. Peter and Andrew's boat was probably moored in front of the house. Herodian era oil lamps found here helped to establish the date. It was found that the original home was enlarged about 50-years after the resurrection. It was plastered and converted into a home church (*domus ecclesia*). Graffiti from the third and fourth centuries had Christian symbolism and prayers to Jesus. This demonstrates that this site was considered sacred by early Christians. Early writings (Egeria c. 380 and the anonymous pilgrim of Piacenza c. 570) attest to the belief that the church in

Capernaum was built over the home of Simon Peter. It cannot be absolutely confirmed, but it is likely that this was Peter's house.

If, as the evidence and tradition attest, this was Peter's house, then it was extremely likely that the church in Capernaum would have started here. That means that the earliest Christians in Capernaum, and possibly in all Galilee, met and worshiped on this site. The earliest baptisms probably took place in the Sea of Galilee just a few steps away. The 5th century addition to the Byzantine church included a baptistry on the south side with steps down into it affirming both baptism by immersion and adult baptism. So, on this site shortly after Pentecost, people were worshiping, being baptized in the name of Jesus Christ and receiving the gift of the Holy Ghost. It is interesting to speculate how long the original pattern of the church was followed before becoming diluted by politics and government recognition which eventually pressured even the people in this holy place to change their mode of baptism. At some point in the history of this local church, people stopped speaking in tongues and being baptized in Jesus' name.

10

Chorazin Χοραζίν (*Furnace of Smoke*)

This New Testament town was founded in the first century. It was an agricultural town famous for its wheat. The water supply was from a spring in the town's northeast. Additional cisterns were built under houses. An oil press was found on the western side close to the road that connected Chorazin with Capernaum. Most of the visible ruins are from the third and fourth centuries A.D. Buildings here, even the synagogue, were made of local black basalt stone.

Synagogue

The stones standing today are from the synagogue built in the 4th century. Recent excavations have found evidence of the 1st century synagogue that Jesus taught in under the 4th century remains. The entrance of the synagogue faces south towards Jerusalem. The wide staircase leads to a small court in front. There were three entrance doors in this front. Part of the decorative gable can be found in the court. It would have been situated directly above the larger, central door. The five columns inside the synagogue remain of the twelve original columns which held up the ceiling and roof.

Cathedra of Moses

Beside the main door of the synagogue is a replica of "the seat of Moses." (The original is in the Israel Museum in Jerusalem.) The Aramaic inscription on the seat says, "Be remembered for good Yudan, son of Ishmael, who made this stoa and its staircase. As his reward may he have a share with the righteous." This is probably where the priest or elder would sit to judge the people. Jesus said, "The scribes and Pharisees sit in Moses' seat (Gr. *kathedra*: the exalted seat occupied by men of eminent rank): All therefore whatsoever they bid you observe, that observe and do" (Matt 23:2, 3).

Mikveh (Mikvah)

On the north side of the synagogue is a mikveh, or ritual bath, covered by a series of long stones. Ritual cleansings, not unlike baptism, were performed at mikvehs found all over Israel. A cistern is beside the mikveh (with an iron grate). Observant Jews still use mikvahs, males on Fridays (before the Sabbath) and before major religious holy days, and females before their wedding, and following childbirth and menstruation. Conversion to Judaism requires one to submerge entirely in a mikvah.

Jesus' Prophecy

As you walk among these ruins, imagine a vibrant city with laughing children running between the houses, shopkeepers selling their wares, the oil press in full operation, travellers stopping for a lunch of warm bread made from local wheat and fish from Capernaum. See a crowd of people ascending the steps to the synagogue, men and women gathered in groups excitedly discussing the miracles that have been happening. This was a successful town. It was prosperous. It was safe. There were no walls. There was peace in the land under Roman rule. It was home.

Jesus taught in this synagogue. He healed many and performed miracles. But the people did not change their lifestyle. The did not repent.

> Then began he to upbraid the cities wherein most of his mighty works were done, because they repented not: Woe unto thee, Chorazin! woe unto thee, Bethsaida! for if the mighty works, which were done in you, had been done in Tyre and Sidon, they would have repented long ago in sackcloth and ashes. But I say unto you, It shall be more tolerable for Tyre and Sidon at the day of judgment, than for you (Matt 11:20-22).

Jesus included Capernaum in his rebuke. It's amazing that after 2,000 years, some other 1st century towns continue to exist (Tiberius, Nazareth, Jerusalem, Joppa, Hebron and many more). But the three towns closest to the center of Jesus' ministry in Galilee are ruins and ghost towns. In fact, after many years of excavations, they are just beginning to think they might have found where Bethsaida was located.

Romans 2:4 says, "the goodness of God leadeth thee to repentance." Signs, wonders, healings and miracles should persuade anyone to follow God, and they point toward repentance. They should make a person want to repent. But all of these can only "lead to repentance." God leads. He doesn't force repentance. Repentance that is forced is not true repentance. Remain sensitive to the leading of God. Respond to His goodness, lest, like Chorazin, you become a wasteland and a pitiful picture of what used to be.

11

Hazor חָצוֹר (*Castle*)

Tel Hazor is the largest archeological site in Israel. Located to the north of the Sea of Galilee, on a major trade route connecting Egypt and Babylon, Hazor was the largest and most important city in Canaan when Israel entered the promised land. It was ten times larger than Jerusalem (Jebus) with a population of 15,000 to 20,000. It was "the head of all those kingdoms" (Joshua 11:10). Archeologists discovered evidence of the destruction of Hazor by fire in the 15th century B.C. and again in the 13th century B.C. This corresponds with the destruction by Joshua (15th century B.C.) seen in Joshua 11:10, 11 and the later destruction by Deborah and Barak in the 13th century B.C. as witnessed in Judges 4:23, 24. The burn line is still visible as an ash layer in certain areas of the site.

After its destruction by Israel, it was rebuilt and inhabited by Israelites, probably during the reign of Solomon. Finally, it was destroyed by the Assyrians under Tiglath-Pileser III in 732 B.C.

Jabin, King of Hazor

Critics have attacked the biblical record by pointing to mention of "Jabin, King of Hazor" during the conquest by Joshua in Joshua 11:1, and "Jabin king of Canaan, who reigned in Hazor" a century and a half later in Judges 4:2. Archeology has shed light on this confusion. In 1992, a tablet was discovered at Hazor addressed to "Jabin, the King of Hazor" which dates to the 17th or 18th centuries B.C. Another tablet from the Mari Texts had been discovered earlier naming Jabin as king of Hazor. Thus, "Jabin" is more of a title than a name. It was applied to kings of Hazor over a period of 400 years, similar to the title, "Pharoah, king of Egypt."

Solomonic Gates

The six-chambered gate, very similar to that at Megiddo, dates from the time of Solomon. These gates are in much better condition than those at Megiddo and date from the 10th century B.C.

Throughout the remainder of this 200-acre site are the remains of Canaanite buildings, some of them lined with orthostats, a water shaft similar to that seen at Megiddo, a storehouse or stable with tripartite pillars and a typical four-room pillared house used by Israelites from the time of their settlement throughout Israel. These houses are characterized by one or two rows of pillars that separate the central court from the side rooms.

Grand Staircase

One of the most amazing discoveries at Hazor was the Grand Staircase discovered in 2018 during the ongoing excavations. The 14-foot-wide staircase is unique in its craftmanship for this era and region, with each step shaped to fit in a manner not found elsewhere. The first seven steps, possibly leading into a palace, were found and restored. Further excavations will reveal the remaining staircase.

12

Dan דָּן (*Judge*) (named for the father of the tribe of Dan)

Originally known at Laish or Leshem, this was a large and strong Canaanite city by the 18th century B.C. High walls protected the city on all sides. Within its boundaries are two springs, Dan and Leshem, which combine to form the largest of the three sources of the Jordan River. By the 12th century B.C., they lived peaceably and had no known threats. They probably welcomed the five spies from the tribe of Dan further south. Big mistake. They apparently paid little attention to security. Though they lived behind massive walls, they probably left the gates open. Another mistake. The five spies brought 600 families, took over the city and renamed it after their father. From that time, the length of Israel was referred to as "From Dan to Beersheba." Judges 18 tells this story as well as how the Danites stole Micah's gods and priest and began practicing idolatry in their new home.

The House of David

Until 1993, critics contended that the story of King David was myth. They said there was absolutely no proof that Israel ever had a king named David. But in 1993, here at Tel Dan, a stone slab or stela was discovered with clear and precise writing in Aramaic that mentions a king of the House of David. It is the victory declaration of an Aramean king boasting of his victory over the "king of Israel" and the "king of the House of David." Most biblical scholars and archeologists now concede the historical existence of King David of the Bible.

The Israelite Gate

Approach the city through a large paved open space. Enter through the Israelite-style outer gate and inner gate. Directly in front of you as you come through the gate is a raised platform surrounded by round, decorative stones with grooves in the tops that held poles for a canopy. This may have been for a judge or a king. "Then the king arose, and sat in the gate. And they told all the people, saying, Behold, the king doth sit in the gate. And all the people came before the king" (2 Sam 19:8). Beside the platform and alongside the wall is a stone bench where the elders of the city would sit as in Ruth 4:1.

The High Place

By the time of Jeroboam, the breakaway king of Israel's northern 10 tribes, Dan was ready to accept one of the two golden calves made to keep people from worshipping at Jerusalem. Just beyond the reconstruction of the four-horned altar is a 25-foot-wide set of stairs ascending to a platform where the golden calf was probably placed. To the sides of the platform and around the area are houses for the priests which were not the sons of Levi but of the lowest sort of people (1 Kings 12:28-31).

The Abraham Gate

This impressive gate is the oldest intact mud-brick gate in the world. The stone steps ascend to this gate to allow the traveler to pass through three arches of sun-baked bricks. The archway is one of the earliest complete standing arches in the world. This is called "Abraham's Gate" because Abraham would have passed this gate during his pursuit of the four kings of the north. He "pursued them unto Dan" (Gen 14:14). The existing gate may have been rebuilt a couple of hundred years after Abraham's visit. As Abraham passed the massive walls of this city, did he ever imagine that his offspring would one day inhabit this place?

Abraham's Gate—Premier Bible Land Photo

Six-Day War Trenches

In 1967, this was the frontier between Israel and Syria/Lebanon. Trenches here were used by Israeli troops during that war.

13

Caesarea Philippi Καισάρεια (*Caesar* or *Severed*) and Φίλιππος (*Fond of Horses*)

It was said that Julius Caesar was born by being 'severed' from the womb, hence our use of the term caesarian birth. The name of this place instantly grabs our attention because it is associated with the conversation between Jesus and his disciples regarding His identity. This is where Simon Peter answered by revelation, "Thou art the Christ, the Son of the living God," and Jesus responded by giving him the keys to the kingdom of heaven (Matt 16:13-19).

Time of Hebrew Conquest

First associated with the worship of Ba'al, this may have been the place identified as Baal-gad and Baal-hermon in Judges 3:3 and 1 Chron 5:23. When the tribe of Dan captured the city of Laish (renamed "Dan"), the influence of this cultic center so nearby might have contributed to their own idolatry and the toleration in their city of the golden calf (Judges 18:27-31, 1 Kings 12:28-30). After the conquest of the east by Alexander the Great in 333 B.C., this became Panias, named after the god Pan who was worshipped by Greeks as the god of goats, hunting, victory in battle and sexual/spiritual possession. Pan was thought to win battles by instilling *panic* in his enemies. He was depicted as half-man and half-goat often playing the flute with which he made goats to dance.

Greek Era

Panias was the site of a battle for control of the region between the Ptolemaic Greeks (Egypt) who built a cultic community here in the 3rd century B.C. and the Seleucid Greeks (Syria) in about 200 B.C. The Seleucids, under Antiochus the Great, won, giving control over this land to the Seleucid dynasty who stopped temple sacrifices in Jerusalem in 167 B.C. Although the Hasmoneans controlled Jerusalem beginning in 140 B.C. and ruled most of Israel from 110 B.C. until the Roman era (and even later as a client state of Rome), Panias may have remained under Seleucid control until the Greek era ended with Roman hegemony throughout Syria in 64 B.C.

Roman Era

Herod the Great was a political animal. He received his power from Rome by fawning on whoever seemed to be the most powerful. After the death of Julius Caesar, the rule of Rome seemed like it might go to Caesar's friend, Marc Antony who had married Caesar's girlfriend, Cleopatra of Egypt. Herod backed Antony. When he was building the Temple in Jerusalem, he built a citadel overlooking the Temple, and named it Antonia Fortress in honor of Antony. In choosing to back Marc Antony, however, Herod put his money on the wrong horse. After Octavian defeated Antony, Herod hastened to Octavian (who later became better known as Augustus) to pledge his loyalty. His audacity impressed Octavian, who allowed him to remain king over Judea and gave him the city of Panias as well as other possessions.

Herod renamed the city Caesarea in honor of his new patron. Shortly thereafter, Herod hurried to build in the honor of Augustus. One of the projects he built to secure favor with Augustus was the temple of Augustus at Panias. The Caesars were considered divine and were worshipped as such, especially during their lifetimes and the reigns of their offspring. The remains of the Augustus temple can be seen directly in front of the grotto. After Herod's death, and the division of his kingdom among his three sons (with Roman approval), Herod Philip, also known as Herod II, inherited this area and made Panias his capital. This is why it was known in Jesus' day as Caesarea Philippi.

ARTIST IMPRESSION OF THE SANCTUARY OF PAN

הצעת שיחזור למתחם המקודש לאל פאן

LEGEND

1 THE TEMPLE OF AUGUSTUS
2 THE GROTTO OF THE GOD PAN
3 THE COURT OF PAN & THE NYMPHS
4 THE TEMPLE OF ZEUS
5 THE COURT OF NEMESIS
6 THE TOMB TEMPLE OF THE SACRED GOATS
7 THE TEMPLE OF PAN & THE DANCING GOATS

מקרא

1 מקדש אוגוסטוס
2 מערת האל פאן
3 רחבת האל פאן והנימפות
4 מקדש זאוס
5 חצר נמזיס
6 מקדש קבר העזים הקדושות
7 מקדש פאן והעזים המרקדות

Temples and Plazas

This entire area, backed by the cliff face, is known as the sanctuary because it was all dedicated to the worship of various gods. The areas of worship will be described as though you are facing the grotto, beginning with the first one on the left and working our way to the extreme right. Many of the ashlars (worked stones) were taken from the walls of these temples and used in the construction of other buildings, including Byzantine churches in the area.

Grotto of Pan

The large open cavern was known as Pan's Grotto, from which the river Hermon used to spring in a great rush. The depths of the spring were said to be unfathomable, literally immeasurable. This is one of the main headwaters of the Jordan River and sources for the Sea of Galilee. An earthquake shut off the gushing flow from the grotto, moving it to come gently from the foot of the mountain. The same earthquake probably reduced the size of the grotto. This was supposed to be where Pan lived. In 2020, an altar was discovered within the walls of a rare c. 400 Byzantine church that was built on a Roman-era temple to Pan. The Greek inscription on the 2nd or 3rd century altar says that Athanaeus, son of Susipater, came all the way from Antioch to fulfill a vow in funding and dedicating an altar to Heliopolitanus Pan. This was a combination of two deities, Pan and Heliopolitanus who was also known as Jupiter or Zeus.

Temple of Augustus (c. 20 B.C.)

Facing the grotto, the first temple directly in front of the grotto was long thought to be the Temple of Augustus. (A more recent find in nearby Khorvat Omrit also bears resemblance and may actually be the Augusteum. More research is required to settle the question.) Semicircular niches along the western wall held statues (possibly of Augustus).

Court of Pan & the Nymphs

East of the Grotto of Pan, located between two temples, is the Court of Pan and the Nymphs. A large niche in the wall of the cliff at the rear of the court was for a statue of Pan. A smaller niche above it, decorated with a seashell motif, may have been for the nymph Echo. An inscription in Greek between the two niches is dated from 87 B.C. and says, "The priest Victor, son of Lysimachus, dedicated this goddess to the god Pan, lover of Echo." Another niche is located a few feet to the right and may have been for a statue of Pan or Hermes. Still a fourth niche further to the right has a shell decoration inside its top and Greek inscriptions to either side.

Temple of Zeus

To the right of the Court of Pan & the Nymphs was the temple of Zeus. This was a grand temple located in the center of the sanctuary and dates from the time of Trajan (98-117 A.D.). One of the columns, with a Corinthian capitol, survives at the southeast corner of the temple.

Court of Nemesis

Adjoining the temple of Zeus to your right, is the long, narrow court of Nemesis, the Roman goddess of imperial justice and vengeance. This court dates from 178 A.D. The floor leading to the cliff face is paved with pink and white stones laid in a checker pattern. The large niche in the cliff face at the back of the court contained a statue of Nemesis as described by the Greek inscription. A paved floor leads from the court of Nemesis to the Temples of the Dancing Goats.

Temple and Tomb of Sacred Goats

To the right of the court of Nemesis, and the eastern extreme of the sanctuary, were two temples built about 220 A.D. The upper structure, against the cliff face, is the Tomb Temple of the Dancing Goats. This was an actual tomb where the bones of sacred goats were kept, along with offerings of silver and gold coins, and glass and pottery vessels. There is a niche in the cliff face above this Tomb/Temple. The lower temple, in front of the Tomb, was the Temple of Pan and the Dancing Goats. This temple had a semi-circular shape.

Gates of Hell

This term could refer to the entire sanctuary where false gods were worshipped, or specifically to the grotto where the waters emerged from a "bottomless pit." According to some sources, living babies and children were sacrificed by throwing them into these waters. Others believe that demons will come through these "Gates of Hell" to torment the earth in the end time (Rev 9). It is probable that Panias was likened to the "Gates of Hell" because it represented all false doctrine, idolatry and political intrigue and oppression. Jesus was saying, "Nothing this world can throw at you will succeed. The Church will take on all comers and emerge victorious." "Give it your best shot, devil, you will not prevail." Nowhere else is the term "gates of hell" found in the Bible, but Jesus did use similar terminology in His letter to the angel of the church in Pergamos. "I know thy works, and where thou dwellest, where Satan's seat is" and "where Satan dwelleth." These unique and unusual designations both refer to locations that share some common features. Both Banias and Pergamos were cultic centers containing temples to various deities. Pergamos had a massive altar to Zeus and Banias had a temple of Zeus. Perhaps more strikingly, Pergamos was the site of the first temple of Augustus, the first Roman emperor who was deified, while Banias also had a temple of Augustus. This worship of political figures must be considered a contender for the designations of Matthew 16:18 and Revelation 2:13. This recalls Paul's warning of "that man of sin…the son of perdition; who opposeth and exalteth himself above all that is called God, or that is worshipped; so that he as God sitteth in the temple of God, shewing himself that he is God" (2 Thes. 2:3, 4).

This Rock

There was probably a multiple meaning in the Lord's reference to "this rock." First, Jesus was literally playing on Peter's name, "*Petros*," which meant "a stone" or "a piece of rock." Truly, calling Peter a rock upon which He would build His church, accompanied with giving Peter the keys to the kingdom of heaven, would have positioned Peter to be the spokesman on the day of Pentecost at the very birth of the church. Actually, either of the above scenarios would have given Peter the authority that he later used. Both of them together ("in the mouth of two or three witnesses") merely confirmed his authority. Thus, it was Peter, backed up by the other apostles, (literally "standing up with the eleven" Acts 2:14), who answered the prime question: "Men and brethren, what shall we do?" Peter's answer remains the key for entry into the kingdom of heaven. "Then Peter said unto them, Repent, and be baptized every one of you in the name of Jesus Christ for the remission of sins, and ye shall receive the gift of the Holy Ghost" (Acts 2:38). Peter was also present in Samaria with John when they laid hands on those whom Philip had already "baptized in the name of the Lord Jesus…and they received the Holy Ghost" (Acts 8:12-17). And it was Peter who took the gospel to the Gentiles when the household of the Roman centurion, Cornelius, was filled with the Holy Ghost evidenced by speaking with tongues after which Peter "commanded them to be baptized in the name of the Lord" (Acts 10:44-48). If it had been anyone other than Peter, to whom the other apostles witnessed Jesus' words to Peter at Caesarea Philippi, it is doubtful they would have responded as favorably to the reports of Gentiles being converted into the church without first becoming Jews by circumcision and adherence to other Jewish laws. So, in all these ways, Simon Peter was, indeed, a rock and a significant part of the foundation upon which the church was built (Eph 2:20).

However, there was a difference between Peter (*Petros*) and "this rock" (*petra*). Whereas Peter was *Petros* (a stone and a piece of the rock), "this rock" was *petra* (rock, cliff, ledge, projecting rock, crag, a large stone). So, secondly, the rock referred to by Jesus could also have been the "rock" of revelation. That is, the doctrine that Jesus was the Christ (Messiah) and the Son of the living God. This bold statement, revealed to Peter by God, at once acknowledged Jesus as the promised Son of David, for that is who the Christ would be. Everyone recognized that and was looking for a seed of David to rise up to become king of Israel. Public expectations were, however, far short of the plan of God who intended the Christ to be, not only king of the Jews, but also King of kings. Peter expressed this when he added, "the Son of the living God." Thus, not only was Jesus the Son of David, for which He was not persecuted, for He could claim to be David's offspring without proclaiming Himself to be divine. But when Peter blurted out that His true identity was the Son of the living God, he proclaimed Jesus to be divine.

There is a third way of looking at Jesus saying "Upon this rock I will build my church," and that is the possibility that Jesus was stating, "Right here, in this very place, I will build my church. All these temples to false gods will be destroyed, and those gods will no longer be worshipped. But when all these temples are fallen, my church will remain, and I will be worshipped. Upon this very rock where now stands all these temples, will someday stand my church."

I think that when Jesus proclaimed that He would build His church on "this rock," there was a purposeful juxtaposition between the rock of truth and the rock of error which was the overpowering image from Caesarea Philippi. He was positioning His Church against all the false religious and political systems in the world and saying, "All of this will not prevail against My Church. My Church will stand."

Simon Peter at Caesarea Philippi

You and the others stood silently contemplating the temples built into the cliff at Caesarea Philippi. For hundreds of years, idolaters had come here to worship and bring offerings to their gods. Jesus broke the silence, "Who do men say that I the Son of man am?" For once you were not the first to speak. You remained thoughtful, still gazing at the temples made for dead men and gods that were never alive. You heard the others begin to respond, "Some say you are John the Baptist: some, Elias; others, Jeremiah or one of the prophets." You heard them, but you were parsing the question in your mind. "Why is He asking this? It's not like Him to ask us what others are saying. His way is to teach us. What if…" Jesus interrupts your thoughts, "But who do *you* say that I am?" It's almost as if He is talking to you alone. In a flash, words and phrases came unbidden to your mind. Snatches of the prophets and the law. It bubbles up from the depth of your soul. The teachings and meditations of a lifetime begin to come together like flesh on the bones in Ezekiel's valley. Line upon line. Precept upon precept. Here a little and there a little. It comes together in a rush. "Unto us a child is born, a son is given, the government upon his shoulders, his name shall be called wonderful counselor, mighty God, everlasting Father, Prince of peace."* You blurt it out even while it is forming in your mind: "You are the Christ! The son of the living God!" He smiles like the sunshine. "You are blessed, Simon son of Jona, because flesh and blood did not reveal this unto you, but my Father which is in heaven. And I tell you that you are Peter, and upon this rock I will build my church; and the gates of hell shall not prevail against it. And I will give unto you the keys of the kingdom of heaven. Whatever you bind on earth will be bound in heaven, and whatever you loose on earth will be loosed in heaven." You are stunned by His words. Never have you been singled out like this and placed in such a position of authority. For once, you are speechless. The others are too. It was a quiet group that made their way back to Galilee. By the time you arrived, you were feeling pretty good about your new position.

(*The inclusion of Isaiah 9:6 in this story was inspired by a message preached in Calgary by Mitchell Elder in October 2021.)

14

Mt. Hermon חֶרְמוֹן (*Sanctuary*)

> Behold, how good and how pleasant it is for brethren to dwell together in unity!
> It is like the precious ointment upon the head, that ran down upon the beard,
> Even Aaron's beard: that went down to the skirts of his garments;
> As the dew of Hermon, and as the dew that descended upon the mountains of Zion:
> For there the LORD commanded the blessing, even life for evermore (Psalm 133).

Mount Hermon rises in three countries, Israel, Lebanon and Syria. Though the mountain soars to over 9,000 feet (in Syria), the highest point in Israel is over 7,000 feet. It is the only place with snow skiing in the country. Mt. Hermon provides the backdrop for views north from the vicinity of Galilee. More than twenty ancient temples have been found on Hermon's slopes. This was the "high place" of all high places in the land. It was known more recently as "the eyes of Israel" for the radar emplacements near the top. Hermon is the source of all tributaries of the Jordan River that flows into the Sea of Galilee.

15

Bethshean שְׁאָן בֵּית (*House of Ease*) (Beth Shan, Beit She'an)

Given to the tribe of Manasseh, Bethshean remained a Canaanite city well into the kingdom age. It is strategically located at the confluence of the Harod and Jordan rivers and is at a main junction of those two valleys. It controlled traffic between the Jordan Valley and the coast as well as between Jerusalem/Jericho and the Galilee, and beyond to Damascus. The most ancient town was located on top of the hill, providing a strong, defensive position.

Archeological examinations date the earliest settlements as well before the Bronze Age. Canaanite graves dating from 2000-1600 B.C. were discovered on the mound. After conquest by Thutmose III in the 15th century B.C., the town on the summit became the administrative center for Egypt in this area. Steles[3] and other Egyptian artifacts from the period have been found and are in the Israel museum. The entire site was destroyed by fire during the collapse of civilizations around 1177-1150 B.C.

The Hellenistic period saw a repopulation of Bethshean under the name "*Scythopolis*." Under the Romans, Bethshean was the main city of the Decapolis (the ten cities) and the only one west of the Jordan. It continued to grow during the Roman and Byzantine years, reaching its maximum population of about 40,000 in the

---

[3] steles; cut or prepared stones or pillars bearing inscriptions.

sixth century. By that time, it was predominately Christian with smaller Jewish and Samaritan populations. Byzantine forces were defeated in 634 A.D. and the city came under Muslim rule where Christians and Muslims lived side by side. The city was completely destroyed by earthquake on January 18, 749 A.D. It never recovered its former glory.

When Saul and the army of Israel were defeated on the slopes of Gilboa, the Philistines brought his armor here to display in the temple of Ashtaroth. This may have been the same armor David tried on before facing Goliath in the Valley of Elah (1 Samuel 17:38, 39). It possibly included "the shield of Saul, not anointed with oil" (2 Samuel 1:21). The bodies of Saul and his sons were hung on the walls of Bethshean.

> And when the inhabitants of Jabeshgilead heard of that which the Philistines had done to Saul; All the valiant men arose, and went all night, and took the body of Saul and the bodies of his sons from the wall of Bethshan, and came to Jabesh, and burnt them there. And they took their bones, and buried them under a tree at Jabesh, and fasted seven days (1 Sam 31:11-13).

Jabeshgilead, about seven or eight miles to the east, on the other side of Jordan, was the site of Saul's first battle and victory as king of Israel. It was because of Saul that the men avoided having their right eyes put out by the Ammonites as recorded in 1 Sam 11. Jabeshgilead was also the only community of all Israel that did not participate in the near total destruction of the tribe of Benjamin in the ugly story found in Judges 21. Because they did not join in the destruction of Benjamin, Israel destroyed Jabeshgilead except for

400 young virgins. These 400 young women were given as wives to 400 of the only surviving 600 Benjamites. Therefore, two-thirds of all Benjamin at the time of Saul were descended from the women of Jabeshgilead. It is likely that these Jabeshgileadites were in fact, Benjamites. This might explain why Saul rushed to their defence early in his reign, and why they risked their lives to rescue the bodies of Saul and his sons from the shame and mockery at Bethshean.

Mound and Ruins of Bethshean—Photo Credit Amy Doty

16

Jordan Valley יַרְדֵּן (*Descender*)

This journey assumes travelling the Jordan Valley from north to south, or from the Sea of Galilee to the Dead Sea. If entering the valley at Bethshean, the first few sites will be by-passed.

Degania Dam

Built in the 1930s as a hydroelectric power plant, the small dam at the southern end of the Sea of Galilee regulates the water levels in the Sea and flows into the Jordan River. The existence of this dam may help explain why the stone jetties at ancient Capernaum remain under water.

Degania Alef

Immediately past the dam on the right, on Hwy 90, is Degania Alef, the first kibbutz in Israel. It was started in 1910 under Ottoman rule with eight men and one woman. Gideon Baratz, born 31 May 1913, was the first child born on a Jewish kibbutz in the land. (This birth followed by only a couple of weeks the revelation of baptism in the name of Jesus at the Arroyo Seco Camp Meeting.) The second child born on this kibbutz was Moshe Dayan, the one-eyed Israeli general and Minister of Defence during the Six-Day War in 1967.

East Bank

Since we have crossed the Jordan River, we are technically on the east bank of the river for the first few miles of our journey.

Yarmouk River

As you drive south, the Yarmouk River on our left is the largest tributary of the Jordan. Upriver it forms the boundary between Jordan and Syria for many miles. Until the Yarmouk River flows into the Jordan River, it forms the boundary between Israel and Jordan. This happens about 4 miles from the southern tip of the Sea of Galilee. It also forms the natural boundary between the Golan to the north and the mountains of Gilead to the south. One of the most decisive battles in human history was the Battle of Yarmouk which took place near the Yarmouk river, about 20 miles from here, in 636 A.D. It saw the end of Byzantine rule in Syria. It marked the beginning of the great Muslim advance only four years after the death of Muhammad. There were two cities from the Old Testament situated at or near this famous battlefield: Golan, the city of refuge, and Ashtaroth, the capitol of Og, king of Bashan. Ashtaroth was the seat of idolatrous worship of the goddess Astarte or Ashtaroth. Judges 10:6 says, "the children of Israel did evil in the sight of the LORD, and served Baalim, and Ashtaroth, and the gods of Syria…" North of the Yarmouk, to the east of the Golan, all the way to Hermon, is the land of Bashan.

Gadara

About three miles to your left, on the north bank of the Yarmouk, is the hot springs spa town of Hamat Gader, known in the New Testament as Gadara. This is the country of the Gadarenes and apparently spread up to the eastern shore of the Galilee (Mark 5, Luke 8).

Lodebar לֹא דְבָר (*Pastureless, Not a Pasture*)

Where Jonathan's son, Mephibosheth was found when King

David sent for him in this area east of the Jordan (2 Sam. 9).

Ramoth רָאמוֹת *(Ramot: height)*-Gilead גִּלְעָד
Another city of refuge, on the heights about 20 miles east.

Pella (one of the Decapolis), on the first wadi south of Harod and at the foot of the Gilead hills, was said by Epiphanius and Eusebius of Caesarea to be where the Christians fled from Jerusalem before its siege and destruction by the Romans in 70 A.D.

Jabesh-Gilead יָבֵשׁ גִּלְעָד was 3 or 4 miles across the Jordan just south of Bethshean.

Cherith כְּרִית (*A Cut* or *Cutting*) was the intermittent brook where Elijah was fed by ravens until it dried up. It was located in this area east of the Jordan, possibly just past Jabesh-Gilead and Tishbe which some maps show to be on the Brook Cherith. Elijah the Tishbite was from Gilead (1 Kings 17:1). Gilead is this area from the Yarmouk River to the northern shore of the Dead Sea.

Jabbok (Zarqa) River יַבֹּק (*Pouring Forth*)
As you approach the modern village of Marj Naje, look left across the Jordan Valley. See the gap in the distant mountains? That is the valley of the Jabbok, called Zarqa River today. Just past where it enters the mountains is Penuel and Mahanaim. They may actually be the same place. Penuel is where Jacob wrestled with the angel all night long (Gen 32). Abner brought Ishobosheth to Mahanaim and made him king after the death of Saul (2 Sam 2:8). Mahanaim is where King David went when he left Jerusalem

fleeing from Absalom (2 Sam 17:24, 27). Absalom and 20,000 Israelites were killed in the woods on those mountains. Absalom was caught by his head in an oak tree in that forest (2 Sam 18:6-17) and David sat in the gate of Mahanaim when he heard the news of Absalom's death and when he comforted the people (2 Sam 18:24-19:8). Closer, in the flatland between the Jordan and the Jabbok, "In the plain of Jordan did the king (Solomon) cast them (all the vessels that pertained unto the house of the LORD) in the clay ground between Succoth and Zarthan" (1 Kings 7:46). The Zarqa runs into the Jordan immediately past the junction of Hwy 90 and 57.

Succoth יַרְדֵּן *(Booths)*

Succoth, now called Dayr Allah, is directly across the Jordan River where the Zarqa crosses Hwy 65. This is where Jacob came after meeting Esau on his return to the land. It was his first home after he was renamed "Israel." Here "*he built him an house, and made booths for his cattle: therefore the name of the place is called Succoth*" (Gen 33:17). When Jacob left Succoth and crossed over into Canaan, he travelled into the mountains, probably through the Farah Valley (where Hwy 57 goes today) to Shechem. His boys caused him a lot of trouble there (Gen 33:18-20).

Gilgal יַרְדֵּן (*A Wheel* or *Rolling*)

No more than seven miles north of Jericho, Gilgal was Israel's first place to camp after they came across the Jordan, led by Joshua. It was here that Joshua set up the twelve stones taken out of the midst of Jordan (Joshua 4:19-24). They observed circumcision and Passover here for the first time since coming out of Egypt and this is where the manna ceased (Joshua 5). Israel camped here while Jericho was taken, and when Achan was judged following the defeat at Ai. This is where the inhabitants of Gibeon beguiled Israel into making a league with them by an elaborate ruse that they had come many days march (Joshua 9). Saul was made king in Gilgal (1 Sam 11), and it was here that Saul became impatient with Samuel taking it upon himself to offer the sacrifice (1 Sam 13). It was the beginning of the end for Saul. It was here that Samuel rebuked Saul for sparing Agag and hacked the Amalekite king to pieces himself.

> Hath the LORD as great delight in burnt offerings and sacrifices,
> as in obeying the voice of the LORD?
> Behold, to obey is better than sacrifice,
> and to hearken than the fat of rams.
> For rebellion is as the sin of witchcraft,
> and stubbornness is as iniquity and idolatry.
> Because thou hast rejected the word of the LORD,
> he hath also rejected thee from being king
> (1 Sam 15:22, 23).

King David came here after the defeat of Absalom. It was from here that he was escorted back to Jerusalem via the valley that became known as the Jericho road and today as the Wadi Qelt.

God spoke through Hosea (9:15) – "All their wickedness is in Gilgal: for there I hated them: for the wickedness of their doings I will drive them out of mine house, I will love them no more:
all their princes are revolters."

Jordan River

We have been following the Jordan River since leaving Galilee. Many important events occurred along the length of this river on both sides. However, there were significant events that happened at the river itself. After staying in Succoth, Jacob crossed the river to meet Esau. It was here in the same location that the priests bearing the ark stepped into the Jordan, at which the waters were cut off and ceased flowing from this point south while the waters gathered up to the north as though they had been dammed. Israel crossed over on dry ground. Not least in significance is the baptism of Jesus that almost certainly occurred in this area of the southern Jordan. It was here that our Saviour fulfilled all righteousness and became our example in baptism (Matt. 3:13-15).

17

Jericho; יְרֵחוֹ *(Its Moon or Its Month)*

Believed to be one of the oldest inhabited cities in the world, Jericho was called "the City of Palm Trees" in Deut 34:3. It is the lowest city in the world at 825 feet below sea level. At the time of the conquest, Rahab the harlot had a house of ill repute on the wall. She probably advertised her house with a scarlet cord hanging in the window. She is one of the four women appearing in the lineage of Jesus in the first chapter of Matthew.

Elijah told Elisha to wait here at Jericho, but Elisha refused, and went with him to Jordan where Elijah smote the waters with his mantle. They went over together, and Elisha returned to Jericho alone with his mentor's mantle. Just across the Jordan from this place is where Elijah was taken up in a chariot of fire. Elisha healed the waters of this city (2 Kings 2).

There were 350 children of Jericho in the remnant that returned from Babylonian captivity with Nehemiah (Neh 7:36).

Zacchaeus was chief among publicans in Jericho when Jesus called him down out of the sycamore tree and went to his house (Luke 19:1-10).

As Jesus was leaving Jericho for Jerusalem, blind Bar Timaeus cried out and got His attention. He was healed and "followed Jesus in the way" (Mark 10:46-52). They ascended to Jerusalem up the Jericho road.

The road from Jericho to Jerusalem, on the west, passes what has been known as the Mount of Temptation. Halfway up the mount is the Greek Orthodox Monastery of the Temptation. The Bible doesn't say that Jesus went into a mountain after His baptism, but into the wilderness. These mountains are known by the Crusader name, "the mountains of Quarantania," and the "Mount of Temptation" as Mount Quarantania. "Quarantania" is Latin for forty days and refers to the forty days of isolation Jesus spent in His temptation. It is from this word that we get "quarantine."

18

Masada

While Masada was not mentioned in the Bible, at least not by that name, it is important for being one of Herod the Great's palaces and as the site of the Jewish Sicarii zealots killing their families and committing suicide rather than being captured by the Roman Tenth Legion led by general Lucius Flavius Silva during the first Jewish-Roman War c. 73-74 A.D.

Circumvallation Wall

Still visible today, after almost two millennia, is the stone wall built by the Romans to surround Masada. This was to prevent escape as well as to keep reinforcements and supplies from entering. Look for these walls during your gondola ride or after you reach the top.

Siege Ramp

The Romans bridged the western valley with a ramp designed to allow them to assault the fort with a siege tower and battering ram. It probably took two or three months to construct the ramp for the final assault and breakthrough that came on April 16. The massive ramp remains visible from the western side of the summit.

Water System

Scattered throughout Masada are huge cisterns used to store water from the infrequent rains. An elaborate collection system brought rainwater to these cisterns by a series of channels carved into the face of the cliffs.

Pastor Kenneth Bow makes the pre-dawn trek up Masada Snake Path—Photo Credit Amy Doty

Snake Path

Before the Romans built the siege ramp on the western side, the Snake Path was the main access into the fortress. Travelers still climb the Snake Path, generally starting before dawn to escape the daytime heat and to view the sunrise over the Dead Sea. Carry your camera and some water. Stay with your group and on the path. In 2015 a 20-year-old American university student became separated from her group. She wandered away off the path and fell to her death.

Storage Rooms

Remains of large, rectangular storage rooms have been discovered and partially reconstructed. The black lines on the walls signify the extent of reconstruction. The wall below the black lines remained intact and the wall above the black line has been carefully reconstructed from the stones found nearby during excavation. A sealed jar of 2,000-year-old Judean date palm seeds was discovered during excavations and several have been successfully germinated into date palms. They are currently growing, and a male named Methuselah is producing pollen, at Ketura, south of the Dead Sea. There are plans to pollenate and produce fruit beginning in 2022.

Herod's Palaces

Herod built two palaces at Masada. The Western Palace is just south of the siege ramp on the western side of the summit. The Northern Palace is in three tiers on the extreme north of the Masada site. The upper terrace included the king's living quarters and a semicircular portico with an expansive view. The Roman bathhouse was included in the upper portion of the palace. The middle terrace was a decorative circular reception hall. The lower terrace was also used for receptions and banquets.

Masada Shall Not Fall Again

Many IDF soldiers have been sworn in on Masada after hiking up in the dark. They are sworn in during a torch lit ceremony that ends with the declaration: "Masada shall not fall again."

19

Engedi; עֵין גֶּדִי (*Fountain of the Kid*)

Once located on the shore of the Dead Sea, *Ein* (spring) *Gedi* (kid goat) is an oasis due to a continually flowing freshwater spring. First mentioned in Joshua 15:62, Engedi was listed as a city within the inheritance of the tribe of Judah. It is next mentioned, and perhaps most well-known, as the place where David hid from Saul and cut a piece off Saul's robe when he could have killed him (1 Samuel 24). Saul sought David and his men among "the rocks of the wild goats (literally: ibex)" (1 Sam 24:2). It was also known as Hazazontamar and was where the armies of Ammon, Moab and Mt. Seir were encamped as they planned to come against Judah during the reign of Jehoshaphat (2 Chronicles 20). The Lord told Ezekiel that waters would come out from under the threshold of the temple in Jerusalem and flow into the Dead Sea causing it to live. Fishers would stand at Engedi and spread forth their nets (Ezekiel 47).

As you walk beside the streambed toward the lower waterfalls, watch for the conies in the trees and shrubs along the trail. Look in the streambed and across the valley on the cliffs for wild ibex. These might be descendants of the ibex from David's day. Imagine David and his men refreshing themselves by bathing in the waterfall that tumbles into the small pool.

The community here was destroyed during the first Jewish-Roman War in 66-70 A.D.

20

Qumran

Best known for the discovery of the Dead Sea Scrolls, Qumran may have been established during the reign of King Uzziah in the 8th century B.C. 2 Chron 26:10 says, "He built towers in the desert and digged many wells." A water cistern from that period was discovered on the western side of the site. Qumran was resettled and was continuously occupied from possibly the second century B.C. until its destruction (along with Masada) by the Romans in 73 A.D. The size of the settlement is in dispute, with estimates ranging from a permanent population of only 12-20 to a high of 1,400. There are also various possibilities for the existence of Qumran ranging from an Essene community, fortress, commercial center or a significant villa.

Most scholars agree that some form of writing took place at Qumran, a theory that is supported by the finding of the Dead Sea Scrolls in the vicinity and the discovery in the "scriptorium" of several inkwells and ostraca (broken pottery used for writing purposes) with writing on them, including a practice alphabet.

Beginning in 1947, the Dead Sea Scrolls began to be discovered in 12 different caves contiguous to Qumran. The most recent discovery was in February 2017 in what has become known as Cave 12.

Cave 11 is known as where the Temple Scroll, by far the longest scroll, was found in 1956. In total, portions of 21 texts were found here including part of Leviticus, Deuteronomy, Ezekiel, Psalms, and Job.

Cave 11—Photo Credit Amy Doty

21

Dead Sea

The Dead Sea is referred to in the Bible as the Salt Sea and the Sea of the Plain. The lowest place on the surface of the earth, at 1,412 feet below sea level, is the Dead Sea. Because it is ten times as salty as the ocean, no plant or animal life can exist within its waters, hence its name. This hyper salinity makes swimming in the Dead Sea more like floating. (In fact, don't try swimming. Keep your head and face above the water to avoid stinging eyes.) At a thousand feet, it is the deepest hypersaline lake in the world. Its main source is the Jordan River which flows into it just below Jericho. There is no outlet.

The Dead Sea is evaporating at a rapid rate. Because more water is evaporating than flowing into it, the sea is shrinking. The surface area in 1930 was 410 square miles. Today it is 234 square miles. Currently, the water level drops about 3-feet per year. A joint Israeli/Jordanian/Palestinian project has been agreed upon to bring water from the Red Sea, making desalinated water for drinking and piping the brine into the Dead Sea. It was to be completed by 2021.

As you gaze across the sea, especially beautiful at sunrise, imagine the Israelites, led by Moses, on the opposite shore. The eastern shore, today's Jordan, was the biblical Moab, where Balaam was hired to curse Israel during their 40-year journey. There too, at the north side of the sea, was where the plague afflicted Israel for their whoredom with Moabite women. Over there, from Mt. Nebo, Moses had his final view of the promised land.

22

Jericho Road

The Jericho Road is much the same today as it was in the first century when Jesus and his disciples walked it. Stretching from Jericho to Jerusalem, it remains the narrow path along Wadi Qelt. It is a serious 8½ hour hike along its 22-mile route, a journey often split into two days with a stop in the middle for an overnight rest. The bends, curves, and many caves along its route made the narrow path especially dangerous. Thieves frequently attacked and robbed travelers to and from Jerusalem. This fact made Jesus' parable of the good Samaritan especially relevant to his audience in that day (Luke 10:30-35).

St. George Monastery

Clinging from the cliff face about three hours walk from Jericho is a Greek Orthodox monastery that was first established in the 420s, destroyed by the Persians in 614, rebuilt by the Crusaders in the 12th century, abandoned after the Crusader era and rebuilt again by Greek monks toward the end of the 1800s. It is open to visitors but with a strict dress code: no shorts on men, and no trousers of any kind on women. Women must wear long skirts or dresses and modest tops.

23

Southern Wall of Temple Mount

The Southern Wall was the southern extent of Herod's Temple Mount. Like the Western Wall, it was a retaining wall built to support and define the massive extension of the Temple Mount Plaza enlarged by Herod. Unlike the Western Wall Plaza, the Southern Wall has been excavated to the street level of the first century. The Herodian ashlars visible at the bottom of the wall are original from Herod's day and rest upon the bedrock of Mount Moriah.

Southern Steps

The Southern Steps form the grand stairway, a massive 210-feet across, that Jesus and the apostles would have used in their entrance to the Temple. The portion of the staircase that is currently accessible is 105 feet wide. The Crusader tower was built upon the western 105 feet of the original stairway, thus covering it. The Southern Steps are original from the time before the New Testament, with some of them cut out of the bedrock of Mt. Moriah. Because the Southern Wall was more than a retaining wall, and included entryways into the Temple, invaders destroyed much of the wall down to the lowest course of stones, which still remains. As one approaches the wall, using the same stairs Jesus would have used, they can touch the original Herodian ashlar that Jesus and the apostles might have run their hands along. This area was commonly used for addressing people approaching and leaving the Temple. Many scholars believe this is where "the multitude came together" and Simon Peter delivered his Pentecostal message. Take your Bible, and go slowly up the steps, reading the Psalms of Ascent, also known as the Songs of Degrees. They are Psalms 120–134.

> "I was glad when they said unto me, Let us go into the house of the LORD" (Ps. 122:1).

Double Gate

The 39-foot wide Double Gate is approached via the Southern Steps and is the gate that most people used to visit the Temple in Jesus' day. They would go in one side and exit through the other side. Although the façade is not imposing, the vaulted ceiling inside this gate is elaborately decorated and beautiful. This was most likely the Beautiful Gate where the lame man sat begging for alms. He was prohibited from entering the Temple because of his lameness. But after Peter took him by the hand and said, "In the name of Jesus Christ of Nazareth rise up and walk," he leaped up and entered with Peter and John into the temple, "walking, and leaping, and praising God" (Acts 3:1-10).

This gate is mostly obscured today, covered by a Crusader tower that is being used by the Muslims. They access the tower by using the westernmost of the Double Gates. Part of the easternmost gate is still visible from the Southern Steps including the Herodian lintel and relieving arch. Immediately to the top right of the relieving arch is a stone with an inscription that names Hadrian's adopted son and successor (c. 138). Being inserted into the wall upside down shows that it was reused, possibly from the base of an equestrian statue that used to stand on top of temple mount.[4] The inscription is interpreted:

> "To Titus Aelius Hadrianus
> Antonius Augustus Pius
> The father of the fatherland, pontifex, augur
> Decreed by the Decurions"

---

[4] St. Jerome, *Commentaries* on Isaiah 2:28, Matthew 24:15; The Bordeaux Pilgrim, *Itinerary* 7a.

Triple Gate

Two-hundred-fifteen feet to the east of the Double Gate is the Triple Gate. It was 50-feet wide and approached via a 50-foot-wide staircase. This was probably the gate used for a priestly function, perhaps to carry the water from the Pool of Siloam for use in the Temple. The smaller staircase and the more elaborate façade of the triple gate points to a more exclusive entrance than the more common Double Gate.

Place of Trumpeting

At the utmost southwestern corner of Temple Mount is a stone that was found where it had fallen from the pinnacle of the wall. The stone had an indentation carved into it for the priest to stand and sound the trumpet that could be heard all over the Temple and the surrounding area. An inscription on the stone reads, "to the place of trumpeting" and may have been the architect's instructions for the correct placement of this stone. (The original stone is in the Israel Museum and a replica is located below the SW corner.) It was from here that the priest would sound the beginning and ending of Sabbath. It was possibly from here that the priest would view the last wisp of smoke from the Passover lamb ascending off the altar and shout "It is finished!" Only after this was pronounced could all the priests who had completed their duties be allowed to depart from the Temple and return to their homes. This may also have been the "pinnacle of the temple" where Satan tempted Jesus to cast himself down (Matthew 4:5-7).

Simon Peter at the Beautiful Gate

You had come here with John, at the hour of prayer, the third hour after noon. The lame man was there as he had been every day. He saw you coming and as you were about to go into the gate, he asked you and John for money. You didn't have any money, or you probably would have given him some. Instead, you felt the Spirit of the Lord stirring you. You focused your eyes on the man and said, "Look at us." The man straightened as much as he could and held out his cup of coins. His expectations were dashed when you said, "I don't have any silver or gold," and he was left hoping for a few coppers. But you continued as though you didn't notice his disappointment, "But what I have I will give you. In the name of Jesus Christ of Nazareth, stand up and walk." You reached for his right hand and began to lift him to his feet which were immediately healed and strengthened. The man jumped into the air landing on his feet. This man who had never been allowed to go into the Temple went through the Beautiful Gate and up the steps into the Temple walking and jumping and praising God all while holding on to you and John. Everybody saw him and everybody knew him. He had been a daily fixture outside the Beautiful Gate for many years. The crowd came running to where you were standing in Solomon's porch, and you began to preach. You preached until they came to arrest you. But the officers arrived a little too late. Five thousand men had already believed (Acts 3:1-26; 4:1-4).

24

Western Wall

No place on Earth is revered by Jews more than the Western Wall of the Temple Mount in Jerusalem. This portion of the Wall, also known as the Wailing Wall (although the Jews consider this a derogatory term), is on the "must visit" itinerary of everyone who visits the Holy Land. What is this wall? Why is it so significant? Is it really a "must visit" site in Jerusalem? Have you ever wondered how the Western Wall is still standing in spite of Jesus' words that "There shall not be left here one stone upon another, that shall not be thrown down"?

> And Jesus went out, and departed from the temple: and his disciples came to him for to shew him the buildings of the temple. And Jesus said unto them, See ye not all these things? verily I say unto you, There shall not be left here one stone upon another, that shall not be thrown down (Matthew 24:1, 2).

It is deeply moving to observe religious Jews gathering near the Wall to pray, worship and celebrate bar mitzvahs and bat mitzvahs. Black hatted figures stand next to more liberal Jews wearing white kippahs, and soldiers in olive green. Heads bowed, hands outstretched and often bodies swaying, bending at the waist. Across a divider, women cover their legs and shoulders to pray the same prayers. Prayers for Messiah to come. Prayers for prosperity. Prayers for peace.

The Western Wall was, prior to 1967, the only place where Jewish people were allowed to approach the Temple Mount. It consisted of a narrow alleyway where only a few people at a time could gather and pray. A nineteenth century painting by Gustav Bauernfeind illustrates the way it was for hundreds of years. After the 1967 war, Israel leveled the houses that enclosed the Wall and created the Western Wall Plaza, an area large enough to accommodate thousands. They also lowered the ground level, revealing another two courses of Herodian ashlars (worked stones).

Looking at the Wall today, one would see stones from different periods of history. The bottom seven rows of stones were placed during the building project of Herod the Great. (Herod is called "Great" because of his grand building projects, not because of his greatness of heart.) These Herodian ashlars are many feet above the street level of Jesus' time. That means that Jesus and the apostles would never have touched these stones although they would have seen them from the perspective of the street far below. There are 17 layers of stones that go down 43 feet below the level of today's Western Wall Plaza. Some of these stones are visible in a tour of the Western Wall Tunnels that takes one down to the street level of Jesus' day. Above ground, and visible to all who visit the Western Wall are seven levels of the large, mostly rectangular stones from Herod's wall of about 20 B.C. Above the Herodian stones are 4 courses of mostly square stones from the Umayyad caliphs in the 7th to 8th centuries A.D. The Ottoman Empire ruled Jerusalem from 1517-1917 and added 13 layers of smaller stones to the wall. The last three rows of small stones were added shortly before 1967.

The reason this wall still stands, despite Jesus' words that, "There shall not be left here one stone upon another, that shall not be thrown down," is that Jesus was referring to the buildings on top of the Temple Mount, not to the retainer wall holding up the Mount. Because Herod's plans included enlarging the entire mountain upon which the Temple stood, it was necessary to build a massive wall to hold all the dirt that was hauled in. That is what is seen today, not the Temple walls. There is no trace of Herod's Temple. There is "not left here one stone upon another."

Jews pray here because it is the nearest they can get to where the Temple stood. Actually, the closest place to where the Temple was located is inside the Western Wall Tunnels. People still pray there, and one passes them on every walk through the tunnels.

Wailing Wall by Gustav Bauernfeind 1887

25

Western Wall Tunnels

The tunnels that run along the base of the western wall of the Temple Mount are also known as the Rabbinical Tunnels. Extensive excavations continue to reveal rooms and artifacts hidden from view for two millennia. This walk takes us underground to the street level of the time of Jesus along an ancient street, water channel and quarry. You will see the largest stone discovered in the wall, a massive 520 metric tons and 45-feet in length. The ancient street you walk along is paved with Herodian pavement stones. The water tunnel you walk through is a Hasmonean era aqueduct. Almost always you will pass Jewish women praying at a spot thought to be closest to where the Holy of Holies stood during the time of the Temple. At the northern end of the tunnel, before ascending to present day street level, you will walk around an ancient pool (the Struthion pool) that used to be open but now is enclosed.

26

Pool of Bethesda Βηθεσδά (*House of Mercy* or *Flowing Water*)

What probably started as a quarry outside the Sheep Gate north of the Temple to supply stone for the Hasmonean southern extension of Temple Mount became known as the Pool of Bethesda. (Many pools began as quarries.) This area may have already been known as a healing center connected with Serapis probably during the Hellenistic era. By the time of Jesus, this was possibly divided into a southern pool (visible today) and a northern pool. The pool complex was surrounded by porticoes with one in the middle, making the five porches mentioned in John 5. In these porches, John reveals "lay a great multitude of impotent folk, blind, halt, withered, waiting for the moving of the water. For an angel went down at a certain season into the pool and troubled the water: whosoever then first after the troubling of the water stepped in was made whole of whatsoever disease he had. And a certain man was there, which had an infirmity thirty and eight years. When Jesus saw him lie, and knew that he had been now a long time in that case, he saith unto him, 'Wilt thou be made whole?' The impotent man answered him, 'Sir, I have no man, when the water is troubled, to put me into the pool: but while I am coming, another steppeth down before me.' Jesus, saith unto him, 'Rise, take up thy bed and walk.' And immediately the man was made whole, and took up his bed, and walked: and on the same day was the sabbath" (John 5:1-9).

A basilica was built on this site during the Byzantine period with its eastern end on firm ground and its western end built over the pools, with the nave situated over the dam separating the southern and northern pools. Two series of massive arches were added either side of the dam to support the two side aisles of the church. A smaller Crusader church was built atop the ruins of the Byzantine Basilica. No trace of the five porches from the first century have been discovered.

St. Anne's

Next to the Pool of Bethesda is the French Roman Catholic Church of Saint Anne, built by the Crusaders between 1131-1138 over the site of a grotto thought to be the childhood home of the Virgin Mary. It is dedicated to Anne, the mother of Mary. While most Crusader churches were destroyed by Saladin after the 1187 conquest of Jerusalem, this church was converted into a school. The Arabic inscription transcribed as al-Madrasa as-Saladin remains over the entrance. Eventually, during Ottoman rule the building was abandoned. Ottoman Sultan Abdulmedid I presented it to Napoleon III in gratitude for French support during the Crimean War. France claims ownership to this day and French presidents Jacques Chirac and Emmanuel Macron both had an altercation with Israel security officers at the church, refusing to enter the building until the Israeli soldiers providing his security left. The church is famous for its acoustics which are suited to Gregorian chant. Crowds permitting, we always try to sing in this historic building.

27

Shiloh; שִׁילֹה (*Tranquil* also *the Messiah*)

Shiloh was the capital of Israel for the first 369 years after they arrived in the promised land. It was here that Joshua divided the land to the various tribes. During that time, the tabernacle and ark of the covenant remained there. This is where Hannah prayed for a child and Eli thought she was drunk. After Samuel was weaned, he was left here and learned how to discern the voice of God. It was from here that Hophni and Phineas removed the ark and took it into the battlefield where it was captured by the Philistines before it was given back to Israel. The ark never returned to Shiloh. Modern excavations have revealed the actual spot where the tabernacle was erected. See Joshua 18:1-10, 21:1-8, 1 Sam. 1-4.

28

Mount of Olives; זַיִת *Olivet (Olive)*

One of the best views of the Temple Mount is the Mount of Olives across the Kidron Valley to the east, so named for the olive trees that have grown there since the time of king David. The Garden of Gethsemane is on the lower slope of this mountain. Prefiguring Christ's rejection and suffering, 2 Samuel 15:30 records, "David went up by the ascent of mount Olivet, and wept as he went up, and had his head covered, and he went barefoot: and all the people that was with him covered every man his head, and they went up, weeping as they went up."

Bethany, the home of Lazarus, Martha and Mary, and Bethphage were two villages on the opposite slope of Olivet. Jesus spent his last week walking back and forth between Bethany and Jerusalem, including his ride on the colt of a donkey on Palm Sunday. While you walk on the mount or take the road down toward the Garden of Gethsemane, think about accompanying Jesus toward Jerusalem for the last time. Listen closely to His words. This will be His last journey from Bethany. He will only return after His resurrection.

The events in Acts 1:4-12 occurred here, with the disciples watching as Jesus ascended out of their sight after promising them the Holy Ghost. As you stand near the top of the mount, imagine hearing Jesus' last words of instruction and promise, and then see Him ascend on a cloud out of your sight.

From your viewpoint on the Mount of Olives, you are witness to some of the most amazing events in history. That seemingly insignificant little hill across the valley is known to the Jews as the Temple Mount, to the Muslims as Haram esh-Sharif (the Noble Sanctuary) and to the rest of the world as the most troublesome and contested piece of real-estate anywhere. About 4,000 years ago it was known as Mount Moriah. That's when Abraham climbed it with his son Isaac while Isaac carried wood for a fire. After a three-day journey from Beersheba, God guided him purposefully to this exact spot to build an altar. That altar was very possibly built on the spot where the Dome of the Rock stands today. The Dome of the Rock takes its name from a rock under the very center of the Dome. Muslims believe that the prophet Mohammed's winged horse, named Buraq, carried Mohammed here from Mecca and then from here to heaven for his conversation with God, and back to Mecca on the same night. Some believe that the rock was in the Holy of Holies in the Temple and that the indention on the top of the rock was where the Ark of the Covenant rested.

From the right spot, on a clear day, you might be able to see the Dead Sea.

29

Gethsemane; Γεθσημανῆ (*Oil-press* of Aramaic origin)

At the foot of the Mount of Olives, on the other side of the brook Cedron (Kidron) opposite Jerusalem, Gethsemane was a garden where Jesus often went with his disciples. This is where Jesus took His disciples after eating the Passover with them. It's where He prayed, "Not my will but thy will be done" and surrendered Himself to drink the bitter cup. The disciples slept through most of the prayer time until Judas came leading those who would arrest Jesus. This is where Judas betrayed Him with a kiss (John 18:1-12, Matthew 26:30-56, Mark 14:26-52, Luke 22:38-53).

The olive trees in this garden are very old. It's difficult to get a reliable dating on some ancient trees because although the branches and trunk may die off, the roots underground continue to support life. So, even though an olive tree may die because of fire or a besieging army cutting it down to the ground, it might spring forth again. Olive trees become twisted and gnarled with age and show distinct characteristics. Some olive trees are over 4,000 years old. The trees that stand today on the lower slope of the Mount of Olives may have roots that were here when Jesus visited.

Simon Peter in the Garden of Gethsemane

You were tired. It had been a long day and one that was emotionally draining. What had happened in the upper room was still reverberating in your psyche. First, was the strangest Passover supper ever with Jesus declaring that one of you would betray

Him. Then the arguing among the disciples while He had washed your feet. And Judas's disappearance and the hymn singing like the calm after the storm. Finally, the walk across the Kidron to the garden of the olive press.

Jesus asked you, James and John to go with Him a little further into the garden while the others stayed behind. He'd said, "Stay awake while I go pray." You tried. There was certainly enough to think about. But you just couldn't keep your eyes open. Before you knew it, Jesus was standing over you saying, "Simon? Are you sleeping? Couldn't you stay awake one hour? Wake up and pray so you don't enter into temptation." Then He went back to wherever He had been praying. You stood up and began to walk back and forth. You couldn't see Him for the trees, but you could hear the muffled sound of His prayers. It sounded like He was groaning. You felt afraid for Him and didn't know exactly why.

Before long, your weary legs called for a rest, and you sat with your back against an olive tree. You stretched and rocked back and forth, trying to recall how He had taught you to pray. Your rocking gradually slowed, your words slurred and, again, you relaxed against the tree. You dreamed a troubled dream that somehow you had disappointed the Master. He awakened you again and you were startled by His face. It seemed older, strained with traces of blood on it. He shook His head sadly, turned and went back to pray again. And you slept again.

You would never forget that final time. You awoke to Him saying, "Get up! It's time! My betrayer is near." You stumbled to your feet, but while He was still speaking, a mob approached with swords and cudgels. You recognized the face of Judas in the torchlight as he leaned in to kiss Jesus on the cheek. At that, the men grabbed hold of Jesus and started dragging Him away. You reacted without thinking, drawing your sword and striking out at the nearest man. You were aiming for his neck. You got his ear. It was Malchus, the high priest's servant.

There was a lull in the confusion as Jesus spoke. "Put up your sword. If you live by the sword, you will die by the sword. Do you understand that I could call on twelve legions of angels? But if I did, how could the scriptures be fulfilled that this must happen?" As he was speaking, it was like all the action froze except for Him. He reached down and picked up the bloody ear, wiped it off and put it back in its place on Malchus's head. "Why did you come against me at night as though I was a thief? I was teaching every day in the Temple, but you didn't arrest me there."

The spell was broken then. The crowd was furious at the truth of His words. They handled him roughly and looked around for others to vent their anger on. You ran. All of you ran. You ran off into the dark, leaving Jesus in the hands of the crowd.

30

Valley and Brook of Kidron קִדְרוֹן (Cedron - *Dark*)

Inseparable from the history of Jerusalem is the valley that originates just northeast of the old city and runs south along its eastern border. First biblical mention is when king David fled from Absalom, "and the king also himself passed over the brook

Kidron…and went up by the ascent of mount Olivet" (2 Samuel 15:23-39). An elaborate drainage system carried the blood of countless sacrifices from the Temple into the Kidron Valley during the Temple eras. The brook itself is dry most of the time but the valley provides drainage during times of rain, and eventually drains into the Dead Sea.

The Kidron was the line Solomon established that Shemei was forbidden to cross on pain of death (1 Kings 2:37). King Asa destroyed and burnt his mother's idol by the brook Kidron (1 Kings 15:13). Young King Josiah beat down the two altars made by Manasseh and cast the dust of them into the brook Kidron (2 Kings 23:12).

After eating the Passover with His disciples, "He went forth with his disciples over the brook Cedron, where was a garden, into the which he entered, and his disciples" (John 18:1).

Simon Peter in Kidron

You followed "afar off," picking your way through the darkness, trying to stay on the path. You watched as the guards, illuminated by the circle of light made by the torches, manhandled Jesus across the brook that on the morrow would be flowing with the blood of the Passover sacrifices. You were trying to find the courage that burst out of you in the first confusing moments of Jesus being arrested when you drew your sword and slashed out. Perhaps there was a brief hope that the others would rally and begin to fight, creating enough confusion that Jesus could make his escape. Instead, all his disciples forsook him, including you, and ran out into the night. Nobody chased after you. They weren't interested in you. They had come for him.

A brief thought shoved past the trauma of the moment and stood as a phantom in the valley before you. "How ironic," you mused, "King David crossed this brook fleeing for his life during the rebellion of Absalom. And now the son of David is carried across Kidron and back into the city to face his death." Far enough behind to stay in the darkness, you followed to see where they would take him. After they crossed the Kidron, they began to follow the way that ascended up beyond the City of David and on to the high priest's palace. You followed to see the end (Matthew 26:56-58).

31

City of David (Salem, Jebus, Zion, Jerusalem)

The original city of Jerusalem taken by David was a tiny piece of ground on the ridge of the hill extending south of the temple mount. It was bordered by the Kidron Valley on the east and the Tyropean Valley on the west. David expanded it to include approximately 12 acres.

This was Old Testament Jerusalem, earlier known as Salem. Melchizedek, to whom Abraham paid tithes, was king of Salem (Genesis 14:18-19; Hebrews 7:1-4). The city was later called Jebus meaning "threshing place" (Judges 19:10, 11).

Baron Edmond Rothschild bought up 75% of the land over the City of David. (Edmond's son, David Rothschild, provided the financing to build the Knesset in memory of his father.) Excavations on this site by the City of David Society began in 1978. Archeologists have conducted ongoing excavations for several years, discovering pottery dating from the Chalcolithic (Copper) Age about 3,500 B.C. This is the most important archeological site on earth.

Archeologists have discovered the ancient city of Jerusalem and dated its destruction to 586 B.C., when it was finally taken by Babylon. Burn marks, crumbled walls and Hebrew and Babylonian arrow heads affirm the destruction of that time. Other discoveries include:

Canaanite Water Tunnels

Those seeing the underground excavations of the City of David will walk through 4,000 year old tunnels that were dug by the Canaanites to access their water supply. You can run your hand along the pick marks on the tunnel walls. Joab took the city for David by climbing through the "gutter" or the place water was accessed by the inhabitants of the city (2 Samuel 5:6-8; 1 Chronicles 11:6). This was possibly Warren's Shaft, the vertical shaft for accessing water from the Gihon spring that was discovered and named for Charles Warren in 1867.

Stepped Stone Structure

The large, stepped stone structure ascending from the Kidron Valley appears to be at least 3,000 years old. One authority said it dated from the Canaanite times. More recent work strongly suggests it was part of King David's palace. Bullae discovered at the top seem to confirm it was the Davidic royal palace. Just down the slope are the remains of houses that belonged to people who were rich and probably well connected with the palace. One room contains a very rare indoor toilet, the oldest found in Jerusalem.

Biblical Era clay bullae – These were official clay seals used on important documents to certify the identity and authority of the sender. One group of 51 bullae were found in 1982 including some with names and offices of biblical figures. The discovery of these bullae is further confirmation of the accuracy of the biblical record. They were found preserved because they were hardened by the fire that destroyed Jerusalem in 586 B.C. by Babylon.

- "Nathanmelech the Servant of the King" Chamberlain during the time of King Josiah (2 Kings 23:11) discovered March 31, 2019
- "Gemariah the son of Shaphan" was one of the princes mentioned by Jeremiah (chapter 36)
- "Baruch the son of Neriah" who read Jeremiah's book in the ears of the people (chapter 36)
- "Gedaliah the son of Pashur" (Jer. 38:1) discovered in 2011
- "Belonging to Azariah the son of Hilkiah" (1 Chron 6:13)
- "Jucal the son of Shelemiah" (Jer. 38:1) discovered in 2008
- Another bulla was found mentioning the name of Bethlehem, the first archeological evidence from the first Temple period of a city with that name

In 2009, a collection of 34 bullae was found in excavations of the Ophel (2 Chron. 33:14; Neh. 3:26), just between the City of David and the Temple Mount. Among them was a bulla with the inscription, "Belonging to Hezekiah son of Ahaz, King of Judah." This was the first time that the name of a king of Israel or Judah was discovered in a scientific archeological dig in Jerusalem. Another bulla in this discovery reads, "Belonging to Isaiah prophet." Hezekiah and Isaiah were contemporaries.

Gihon Spring

This is the spring that supplied water to ancient Jerusalem and is probably the reason for its existence. The spring originated in the Kidron Valley and was walled in to prevent it from being accessed by enemy troops and to allow all the residents of the city to be able to access it even during times of siege. The Canaanites built a wall around the spring about 4,000 years ago. The remains of this wall have been discovered and uncovered. Solomon was anointed king at the Gihon Spring. Hezekiah then changed the watercourse by having workers start at both ends and meeting in the middle.

Tabernacle of David?

Deep underground, unseen by the light of day since possibly the days of Hezekiah, are four side-by-side rooms carved out of the bedrock of Zion. In one room is an olive press separated by a wall from what could have been an altar with a drain to carry the blood away. Another room has a storage area and a hole drilled through the rock to which animals may have been tied to. Strange "V" shaped marks in the floor are of unknown purpose but might have held the legs of a table for cleaning animals for sacrifice. Between these rooms is another room in which appears to be a stone set up in the manner of Jacob's pillar. One theory is that this is where King David worshipped. It might have been his prayer altar. When later kings commanded that all personal altars be destroyed so that the people would only worship at the Temple, this place was not destroyed. Perhaps, if it was David's altar, it was spared. Rather than destruction, it was buried and forgotten until archeologists uncovered it.

Hezekiah's Tunnel

2 Chron 32:1-4, 30 (2 Kings 20:20) tells of Hezekiah stopping the flow of the Gihon and bringing it straight down to the west side of the City of David. It runs 1,750 feet from the Gihon Spring to the Pool of Siloam. Also known as the Siloam Tunnel, it was discovered in 1838 by Edward Robinson. When Charles Warren walked through it in 1867, he discovered the vertical shaft leading from it into the city, thus its name, Warren's Shaft. In 1880, a 16-year-old boy, Jacob Eliahu, found the Siloam Inscription on the tunnel wall while wading through the tunnel. It was chipped out and is displayed today in the Istanbul Archeology Museum. Israeli media reported in March 2022 that Turkey had agreed to return it to Israel though officials in Turkey deny that. (An interesting aside is that the boy who discovered the inscription was later adopted by Horatio Spafford who wrote the song 'It Is Well With My Soul'. Spafford set up the American Colony in Jerusalem which became the American Colony Hotel, still owned by his descendants. Horatio Spafford died of malaria in 1888 and is buried in the Mt. Zion cemetery.)

First Century Street

A wide first-century street makes its way from the Pool of Siloam to the Temple Mount. Work is ongoing to uncover the street and brace up the ground above to allow visitors to walk these steps. Pilgrims to Jerusalem would undergo ceremonial cleansing at the Pool of Siloam before walking up this street to offer their sacrifices in the Temple.

Drainage Tunnel

Running directly under the first-century street was the storm drain. Similar to walking the street, one can ascend from Siloam to the Temple Mount by walking through the storm drain. Josephus records that 2,000 people hid in this storm drain during the destruction of Jerusalem in 70 A.D. They appeared to have escaped the destruction of the city above until a Roman soldier heard the noise they made through the pavement of the street. Upon breaking up the pavement, the people were discovered and slain. Among other items discovered was a golden bell (complete with chime) from the garment of the high priest.

32

Pool of Siloam Σιλωάμ but of Hebrew origin (*Sent*)

The biblical Pool of Siloam was discovered accidentally during a water line replacement in 2004. Excavations up until 2022 revealed a pool 225 feet wide with steps on the three excavated sides. Following a lengthy legal battle that went all the way to the Israel Supreme Court, it was announced in December 2022 that the remainder of the site would be uncovered during a thorough archaeological project. This is one of the most significant sites in Jerusalem, going back in time to the reign of King Hezekiah and possibly even earlier. Water from the Gihon Spring through Hezekiah's Tunnel feeds into the pool. The original pool was built during Hezekiah's reign in conjunction with the tunnel dug to bring the Gihon Spring totally within the city walls. It was rebuilt during the Hasmonean Time and upgraded during Herod's reign.

John 9:1-11 tells about Jesus healing the blind man by making clay to place in his eyes and sending him to wash in the Pool of Siloam.

The pool was probably destroyed by the Romans in 70 AD. The ensuing years saw it covered by more than 12-feet of silt and gravel washed down the slopes and valley during the centuries of rain. Circular holes in the pavement and stairs around the site were for resting the conical bottoms of amphora used to transport water, possibly for use in the Temple. The First Century Street ascends 377 vertical feet as it goes from Siloam to the Temple Mount. The pool was large enough and close enough to the site of the outpouring of the Holy Ghost on the Day of Pentecost, that it is a possible location for the baptism of the three-thousand converts following Peter's preaching and command in Acts 2:38.

33

Garden Tomb

The site of the crucifixion and burial of Jesus is thought by many Protestants to be what many know as Gordon's Calvary, so called because General Charles Gordon was a major proponent of this location. Set in a quiet garden with the remains of a wine press and a cistern, the presence of an ancient tomb with Christian markings suggested the place where Jesus was buried. The cliff face next to the garden, today a parking lot for busses, resembles the eye and nose sockets of a skull. At least, it did before erosion took its toll. This is certainly the best place to imagine what the garden tomb would have looked like 2,000 years ago. However, scholarship reveals that the tomb dates back some 600 to 800 years before Christ, meaning that it could not be Joseph's "new tomb". As pleasant as it is to visit this garden and remember the death and burial of Jesus, there is very little possibility that this was the place. (See "Church of the Holy Sepulchre.")

Church of the Holy Sepulchre

Although it is demeaned by the infighting of the various Christian groups vying for control, the Church of the Holy Sepulchre is a more likely contender for the actual location of the tomb of Jesus. The crowds of the sincere and the curious, the competition among priests of various sects, the reek of incense and the glitter of gold and brass seem to take away from the peaceful setting that should identify the tomb. However, history and tradition are strong for this (Church of the Holy Sepulchre) being where Jesus was buried nearly 2,000 years ago. In 2017, during restoration work, archeologists were allowed to remove the marble cladding and view the stone slab that was marked by a cross, the first time it was viewed since at least 1555. Samples taken of the mortar above the slab were tested with the result being that the mortar was put in place in the year 335, confirming this was the place Constantine memorialized as the tomb of Jesus. The weight of the evidence points to Jesus being crucified and buried here on April 3, 33 A.D., with the resurrection occurring Sunday, April 5, placing him in the tomb from Friday to Sunday.

34

Upper Room

Also known as the *Cenacle*, from the Latin *cēnō*, for "I dine," the traditional location of the Last Supper is an historic building that has been used in various historic periods as church, mosque and synagogue. The actual age of the building is disputed but some of the ashlars in the walls date to the Roman period, and possibly the Herodian. Because this structure has been destroyed and rebuilt numerous times not much is original other than some lower ashlars in the walls.

Beneath this room is the traditional site of the tomb of King David. There are always Jewish people praying and visiting this tomb. Most experts do not believe David was buried here. 1 Kings 2:10 says, "So David slept with his fathers, and was buried in the city of David." The area known today as Mt. Zion was probably not occupied during David's reign. The City of David was the 12-acre walled city on the southern spur of Mt. Moriah, across the Tyropean Valley from today's Mt. Zion. It is interesting, however, that Peter's message in Acts 2 very possibly places David's tomb in the near vicinity of the outpouring of the Holy Ghost. "Men and brethren, let me freely speak unto you of the patriarch David, that he is both dead and buried, and his sepulchre is with us unto this day" (Acts 2:29).

Strictly speaking, if David was buried in the City of David, as the Bible plainly says, and if the outpouring at Pentecost occurred near his sepulchre, as is implied in Acts 2:29, then the traditional site of the Upper Room is wrong (as is the traditional site of the tomb of David). It is also important to note, though we commonly speak of Pentecost as the "Upper Room experience," or as happening in the Upper Room, the Bible does not say that. That has been assumed by some because the Upper Room is where the apostles had their accommodations when Jesus ascended from the Mount of Olives (Acts 2:13), and it is identified immediately prior to the Acts 2:14 mention that "These all continued with one accord in prayer and supplication, with the women, and Mary the mother of Jesus, and with his brethren."

35

Kidron-Hinnom Valley Overlook

A favorite viewpoint is the easy to miss viewing platform just before Gallicantu (the House of Caiaphas). This is near the junction of the Kidron and Hinnom Valleys. From here one can look toward the Temple Mount and see the approximate location of the Gihon Spring where Solomon was anointed and proclaimed king. By facing in the other direction, another spring would have been in sight, Enrogel, where Adonijah was prematurely celebrating his own ascension to the throne. The two springs were close enough together, though out of each other's line of sight, that the noise of the trumpet and rejoicing for Solomon were heard by Joab and those who were with Adonijah. Adonijah's party broke up with guests fleeing in every direction. Adonijah himself went and caught hold of the horns of the altar (1 Kings 1).

This place, like the Mount of Olives viewpoint, offers a unique vantage of the geography and history of ancient Jerusalem. Many events that happened in both the Old and New Testaments would have been visible from here, including Abraham and Isaac ascending Mt. Moriah (Gen. 22) and Melchizedek going out to meet Abraham after he defeated the four kings (Gen. 14).

36

Gallicantu; *Cock's Crow* (Latin)

Gallicantu is the Latin name of the church that was built on the possible site of the palace of Caiaphas where Jesus was taken the night he was arrested in the Garden of Gethsemane. Archeologists uncovered an ancient, stepped stone street from the Second Temple era leading from the upper city (Mt. Zion) to the lower city (City of David). This was most likely the way Jesus was brought from Gethsemane. Jesus was probably kept in the basement cell until the next morning. See Matthew 26:57-27:2. This is possibly where Peter and John were kept overnight while awaiting judgment for preaching in the name of Jesus in the Temple (Acts 4:1-3). We cannot be sure but seeing that the trial of Jesus took place here, it is possible that this is also where Peter and John were tried. If so, this is where Peter proclaimed, "Neither is there salvation in any other: for there is none other name under heaven given among men, whereby we must be saved" (Acts 4:12).

Simon Peter Denies Jesus

He warned you. Just hours ago, He called your name. Twice. He said your name twice, just like He always did when He was making an important point. "Simon, Simon, behold, Satan hath desired to have you, that he may sift you as wheat." You instantly had a picture of Satan tossing you up into the air, and you falling to the ground. The whole process is repeated over and over until you have been separated from your faith like the shell of a husk is torn from the grain. The shell of you blows away and the faith you used to have lies alone, unattached, unmoving on the ground. You argued, "No, Lord! I'm ready to go to prison with you and even to die with you. I'll never leave you!" He shook His head sadly and fixed His eyes (Oh! Those eyes!) on you. "I tell you, Peter, the cock shall not crow this day, before you will thrice deny you even know me."

Then the hours in the Garden. The arrest. Everyone was scattered, leaving Jesus alone in the hands of His enemies. You followed in the darkness to see where they would take Him. They took Him to the high priest's house, and you followed, blending in with the crowd in the courtyard to see what would happen. It's late and the night air at 2,500 feet is chilled. You push in around the fire to warm yourself. Everyone in the courtyard could see the trial taking place. They watched with interest, but none with more interest than you. More than interest. Yours was no idle curiosity. Your heart pounded in your chest. You willed Jesus to proclaim Himself. To say, "Yes! I am the Son of David and the King of the Jews!" You hoped that this man you had seen open the blind eyes would blind those who accused Him. That this man who had raised the dead would strike all of them dead at once. You knew He could do it. You hoped He would. Instead, He remained silent. Your thoughts skewed between fear and faith. You looked around for a loaf of bread, wondering if you could rush through the guards and thrust it at Him so He could show them all what He could do. You wanted to scream, "Prove yourself!"

Your thoughts were interrupted by a woman who walked by, stopped, and turned toward you. She stooped down to see your face and proclaimed, "This man was also with Jesus!" The icy hand of fear touched your spine and you lied. You didn't even think about it. You just lied. "I'm not with Him." That's when something died within you. You just denied your friend. You blinked hard. Smoke in your eyes. You asked yourself, "What have I done?" You continued to watch the trial feeling numb. After a little while a man said, "You are one of them." Again, the words just rushed out on their own accord. "Man, I am not!" You emphasized it with an oath. Gall rose in your throat, and you thought you would be sick. You swallowed your self loathing, and it went down like poison. You shivered from the cold, or from something that went much deeper than the cold. You were miserable.

You watched Him standing there so alone, so brave. You imagined yourself rushing to His side, wrenching a weapon from one of the guards and leading Jesus to safety, fighting your way through the hostile crowd. Your daydreams were interrupted by another man who stoutly affirmed, "It's true. This fellow was with him for he is a Galilaean." You stood to challenge him. "I don't know what you're talking about!" You began to curse and swear, "I don't know the man!" That's when the cock crowed. There was a moment of silence in response to your vehement cursing. In that silence you glance up at Jesus. He was looking at you. And you remembered what He had said earlier, "Before the cock crow, you will deny me three times." You stumbled blindly away from the fire, pushing uncaringly through the crowd. Out of the courtyard. Down the steps. You careened until you were alone, beyond the reach of a helping hand, swallowed by the darkness. Bitterly, you wept. You wept until you had no more tears and the sobs still issued forth from your broken heart. You wept as you remembered His eyes. You knew those eyes so well. What did they say? Not, "I told you so." They weren't condemning. That was not hatred or condemnation or judgment you saw. It was pain. But not for Himself. He was hurting for you. He felt your pain. His eyes said, "I know what you've done but I love you anyway." In those eyes were the only sign of hope in this Godforsaken, hopeless night.

Another Chance

You were back, but this time you were with John, both of you with your hands bound as the officers hustled you along the streets that led from the Temple and up the steps to the high priest's house.

It had been an eventful day. You and John had gone to the temple at 3:00 in the afternoon to pray. As you walked up the southern steps and were about to enter through the Beautiful Gate, a lame beggar asked you and John for money. You had seen him here before. He was here every day. And you had given him money before. That's why he was focused on you. But today, you didn't have any money on you. Your heart went out to the lame man and compassion rose within you. Time slowed as you recalled Jesus healing the lame man at the pool of Bethesda, just the other side of the temple. With a shock, you heard the Master's voice in your consciousness. "Verily, verily, I say unto you, He that believeth on me, the works that I do shall he do also; and greater works than these shall he do; because I go unto my Father. And whatsoever ye shall ask in my name, that will I do, that the Father may be glorified in the Son. If ye shall ask any thing in my name, I will do it" (John 14:12-14). You heard yourself say, "Look on us," and the man held out his hand expectantly. Then, with total confidence in the words of Jesus, you said, "Silver and gold have I none; but such as I have give I thee: In the name of Jesus Christ of Nazareth rise up and walk." Then you took the extended hand and lifted him up. The full weight of the man that you felt at the first seemed to immediately disappear as he leaped up and stood on his own.

There was a moment of silence as the crowd took in what had happened. Then they began to shout to one another and beckon to those who had not been close enough to see. The beggar was going through the gate and climbing the steps up to the temple area for the first time in his life. He was walking entirely unaided, leaping and praising God. You headed toward Solomon's porch and the crowd moved with you. Shortly, several thousand men were straining to see and hear what was going on. You felt the presence of Jesus and began to preach.

As you were preaching, the captain of the temple, accompanied by the priests and the Sadducees, pushed through the crowd and forcibly detained you. They led you away toward the palace of the high priest, but they were just a bit too late. Five-thousand men had already believed. It was a ten-minute walk, and your mind flitted from thought to thought like a hummingbird going from one honeysuckle blossom to the next, never settling down in one place. You laughed out loud when you remembered the lame man leaping and rejoicing. The guard looked at you in surprise and then gave you a hard shove just for good measure. But that could not dampen your joy. You looked at John, and in the dimming light could see a smile on his face also. You felt the afterglow of the anointing, knowing that God had used you and that your preaching had been inspired and accepted.

But as you drew near to the high priest's house, other thoughts came unwelcome into your mind. This was the scene of your greatest shame. You saw the silhouette of the palace, the lighted windows staring out accusingly. You began to climb the stone steps and looked over where you had warmed your hands by the fire on the night of Jesus' betrayal. Tears stung your eyes as you remembered your denial, your oaths, your cursing, and the look Jesus gave you when the rooster crowed. Even though you knew that you were forgiven, your head hung down as you were pushed roughly into the palace toward the holding cells. The smile that had lit your face a few moments ago, and the joy that had filled your heart, had been replaced with a deep sorrow that the memories had brought.

The guards tied a rope around your body, under your arms, and let you down through a hole into a dungeon carved out of the rock. They lowered John the same way. After shouting abuse and threats, your escort departed. They were going to supper, and you were going to wait in the dark, without food or drink, until the council would gather tomorrow to judge you.

John, ever sensitive, reached through the dark and grabbed your arm. "Are you alright, Simon? I think we will be ok." You sighed. "Yes, John. I'm ok. And I'm not worried about tomorrow. It's just that this place brings back memories. I'm remembering my failure."

And then you laughed. "Do you remember what I had told him that night before everything happened, and the Lord warned me that I would deny Him? I said, 'Lord, I am ready to go with you to prison and to death.' And here I am. Here we are. John! Do you realize Jesus probably spent that night in this same cell?"

John whispered, "Peter, He's here right now. He is here with us. I can feel Him."

You could feel the chill bumps tickle your spine. Yes! You could feel Him too. You relaxed. Both of you sat on the cold floor with your backs against the wall. It was dark, cold and uncomfortable, but you felt strangely warmed and comforted. You and John talked about what had happened that dark night when Jesus spent his last night in this very cell. After you had gone over every painful detail, you switched gears and began to discuss what had just happened a few hours ago with the lame man as you were going into the Temple. A warm glow filled your hearts and, as you talked, somehow you both fell into a restful sleep.

You awakened to the angry shouts of the guards. It seemed as if you must have had a better night's sleep than they did. You and John were pulled up through the hole and taken to where the council was assembled. You recognized many of these faces. This was the same group of men who had found Jesus guilty of blasphemy in this same place, judging him worthy of death. You and John were placed in the midst of them in an obvious attempt to intimidate you. The man who had been healed had been brought and was standing with you. John smiled at him, and you could feel him relax. You glanced down at the floor. This was the exact place Jesus had been standing. You lifted your head and looked out into the courtyard. And there was the exact place you sat warming your hands by the fire.

The examination began. "By what power, or by what name, have ye done this?" You looked again to the spot in the courtyard where you had denied your Lord. You felt a surge of emotion and glanced at your hands. Steady as a rock. You lifted your eyes and faced these men who had intimidated you on that dark, lonely night that seemed so far away. You could feel the comfort and boldness of the Holy Ghost.

You responded, "Ye rulers of the people, and elders of Israel, If we this day be examined of the good deed done to the impotent man, by what means he is made whole; Be it known unto you all, and to all the people of Israel, that by the name of Jesus Christ of Nazareth, whom ye crucified, whom God raised from the dead, even by him doth this man stand here before you whole. This is the stone which was set at nought of you builders, which is become the head of the corner. Neither is there salvation in any other: for there is none other name under heaven given among men, whereby we must be saved" (Acts 3 & 4).

37

Valley of Elah אֵלָה (*Terebinth Tree* also *Oak Tree*)

This valley was an important passage between the Philistine cities on the coast and the Judean cities including Bethlehem and Hebron. It was necessary for Saul to stop the Philistine army here in order to prevent them from attacking Bethlehem. David and his family knew what might happen if he failed. In this small valley, below Azekah where "the Philistines stood on a mountain on one side, and Israel stood on a mountain on the other side", the fate of Bethlehem and of Judah stood in the balance. It was from this brook, today called *Nahal HaEla*, dry during the summer, that David selected five smooth stones. The events of that day changed the course of history for David and for Israel (1 Samuel 17). (See the article about Azekah.)

38

Azekah עֲזֵקָה (*Dug over, tilled*)

The first mention of Azekah in the Bible is during Joshua's victorious southern Judea military campaign (Joshua 10). Joshua had chased the Amorites from Gibeon to Beth-horon and down the valley of Ajalon (where he had commanded the sun to stand still), all the way to Azekah where the Lord sent hailstones upon them. Located atop a hill, as were many ancient cities, Azekah provides a spectacular view of the Valley of Elah where the decisive battle between David and Goliath took place. Azekah was in Philistine possession and only five miles from Gath, Goliath's home. The Philistines occupied this mountain, and the Israelites were encamped on the mountain across the narrow valley and the brook which flows during the rainy season. The Valley of Elah marked the boundary between the Israelites and the Philistines. It is not hard to imagine the inhabitants of Azekah watching the battle unfold from the safety of their walls and the sides of the hill. Their holiday turned into fear when they saw their champion fall and their armies begin to flee. The Philistines were chased down the valley past Azekah, probably through the low pass just to the south of Azekah, and to Gath and Ekron.

Rehoboam fortified Azekah during his reign (2 Chron 11:9) and it remained a stronghold in Judah until the invasion of Assyrian king Sennacherib. In an extra-biblical text, Sennacherib describes it as Hezekiah's "stronghold, like the nest of the eagle located on a mountain ridge, like pointed iron daggers without number reaching high to heaven. Its walls were strong and rivaled the highest mountains. By means of beaten earth ramps, mighty battering rams brought near with the attack by foot soldiers, my warriors. The city Azekah I besieged. I captured, I carried off its spoil, I destroyed, I devasted, I burned with fire…." (Sennacherib's Letter).[5] Azekah and Lachish were also the last remaining cities of Judah, other than Jerusalem, to fall to the Babylonians (Jeremiah 34:7). It was one of the places where Israelites returning from Babylonian captivity lived (Nehemiah 11:30).

[5] Na'aman, Nadav 1974. "Sennacherib's Letter to God on His Campaign to Judah" Bulletin of the American Schools of Oriental Research. 214.

39

Beersheba בְּאֵר שֶׁבַע (*Well of the Oath*)

Called "The City of the Patriarchs", Beersheba was home to Abraham, Isaac and Jacob. This was where Abraham called home, as much as this wandering man had a home. It was here that he swore an oath with Abimelech that Abraham had dug the well at this place. It was here that Abraham planted a grove and "he called there on the name of the LORD, the everlasting God" (Genesis 22). It was from here that Abraham took two young men and his son Isaac on a three-day journey ending at Mt. Moriah. And it was to this place that they returned after finding in a thicket, a ram to offer unto the LORD.

It was in Beersheba that the LORD appeared to Isaac and where Isaac built an altar, called upon the name of the LORD, pitched a tent and his servants dug a well (Genesis 26:23-25). It was at

Beersheba that Jacob deceived his father and stole the blessing that belonged to Esau. It was from Beersheba that he fled toward Haran and on that journey God spake to him for the first time and promised him all "the land whereon thou liest." Jacob built his first altar, calling it "Bethel" and promised to pay tithes (Genesis 28).

On his way into Egypt with his family, Jacob stopped at Beersheba and offered sacrifices unto God. God spoke to him promising to go with him into Egypt and to bring them out again. This was the last place that Israel and the children of Israel were found in the land promised to them before emerging from slavery a great nation (Genesis 46).

Abraham's Well—Photo Credit Amy Doty

40

Gates of the Old City

Most of the Old City walls and gates visible today were built by the Ottomans during the reign of Suleiman the Magnificent between the years 1537 and 1541. The following will provide brief information about the gates beginning with the New Gate in the Old City's northwest corner and progressing clockwise around the walls.

The New Gate is "New" because it wasn't built until 1889 by the Ottomans to allow access to the Christian Quarter from the outside.

Damascus Gate is the gate where the road to Damascus led out of the city. Beneath this gate is a triple-arched gate dating to the time of Emperor Hadrian c. 135.

Herod's Gate is the easternmost gate in the northern wall which was one of the most vulnerable defences of the city. The Crusader army under Godfrey entered the city through a breach in the wall just east of this gate. It is known as Herod's Gate because of the probably mistaken assumption that the residence of Herod Antipas was nearby. It is also known as the Flower Gate by Jews because of the rosette in the stone above the gate. For many years only a wicket gate (narrow, straight – think John Bunyon's *The Pilgrim's Progress*), was enlarged by the Ottoman's about 1875 to provide access to the new neighborhood developing north of the Old City.

Lions Gate is also known as the Sheep Gate and St. Stephen's Gate because of the tradition that Stephen was stoned just outside this gate. The name "Lion's Gate" comes from the four lions (or leopards) decorating the façade, supposedly placed there because of a dream by the Sultan, warning him to protect Jerusalem and not destroy it. The protruding structure just above this gate is known as a machicolation and was a feature in medieval strongholds used to pour boiling water or oil on attackers from above. This is the only open gate in the eastern wall. The gate was heavily damaged during the Arab-Israeli fighting of 1948 and has been restored.

The Golden Gate is on the east side of the Temple Mount and is considered the holiest gate for the Abrahamic faiths. The location almost certainly matches the location of the eastern gate of the temple which was the only gate in the eastern wall of the First Temple, and remained the most important gate in that wall throughout the time of Jesus. Thus, it was through this gate that the red heifer was led to the Mount of Olives for sacrifice. Also, the scapegoat was led out this gate and into the wilderness to be set free. The term "Golden Gate" was not used in the Bible, but this would have been the gate referred to in Ezekiel 44:1-3. In fulfilment of this prophecy, this was the gate Jesus entered through on Palm Sunday, coming from Bethany and down the Mount of Olives.

The present gate was first built during the Umayyad caliphate which also saw the building of the Dome of the Rock in 691-692. It was built on the foundations of an earlier gate. Two massive pillars found inside the gate survive from the First Temple period. The lowest courses of stones found on either side of the gate are much older than the Hasmonean ashlars above them, dating from before the 6th century B.C.

The Muslims closed the gate in 810 and it was reopened during the Crusader period but closed again when Saladin retook the city in 1187. The Ottomans under Suleiman the Magnificent rebuilt the gate along with the city walls but sealed it up in 1541 and it has remained sealed. The Muslims sealed it to prevent a "false" messiah from entering Jerusalem via the gate and Muslims began burying their dead in front of the gate to discourage any observant Jew from coming through.

The Dung Gate is also known as the Silwan Gate for the neighborhood just to the south, and the Mughrabi Gate because it led to the Mughrabi Quarter, a North African community that used to inhabit the space now used for the Western Wall Plaza. The original gate, built along with the walls by the Ottomans between 1537 and 1541, was very narrow. It was expanded in 1952 by the Jordanians and again in 1984 by Israel. Most visitors who visit the Western Wall come through this gate. This is not the Dung Gate referred to by Nehemiah, as that gate was near the Pool of Siloam.

Zion Gate leads from Mount Zion into the Jewish Quarter of the Old City. Bullet holes from the 1948 Battle for Jerusalem as well as the 1967 Six-Day War are still visible in and around this gate.

Jaffa Gate was built with the wall in 1537-1541 on a possible location of an earlier gate, the Jaffa (or Joppa) Gate faces Joppa and the road leading out of this gate doubtlessly led to Joppa. Bullet marks are visible from the War of 1948. The gate was sealed shut from 1948 until 1967 when Israeli forces took control of the Old City. The tower immediately across the now open street is known as the Tower of David although David had nothing to do with it. It is also known as the Jerusalem Citadel and was first built by the Hasmoneans in the 2nd century B.C. because it was the highest part of the city. Herod build three towers here and one of them, the westernmost, remains in the base of the current tower. Herod's palace was built adjacent and to the south of the towers. Above the gate is the Ottoman inscription surviving from when it was built. It gives the date it was built and credits Suleiman the Magnificent with its building. Another plaque survives in a niche on the other side of the gate.

1.	New Gate	5.	Golden Gate (closed)
2.	Damascus Gate	6.	Dung Gate
3.	Herod's Gate	7.	Zion Gate
4.	Lions Gate	8.	Jaffa Gate

41

Mt. Nebo

The country of Jordan occupies territory of biblical significance and thus qualifies as a Bible Land. (Other modern "Bible Land" countries are Turkey, Greece, and Italy. Special consideration may be given to Malta (Melita) where Paul was stranded for three months on his way to Rome.)

A visit to Jordan typically involves driving over land that was part of ancient Edom, Moab and Ammon. Parts of present-day Jordan, east of the Jordan River, were where the tribes of Reuben and Gad, and the half tribe of Manasseh settled. Many Old Testament events occurred in these lands, some of which are mentioned in Chapter 16.

Historically significant, but not cared for or protected, is one of the earliest purpose-built churches (293-303 A.D.) which was discovered in Aqaba, at the northern end of the Red Sea. Petra, one of the seven wonders of the world, was the capital of Edom before becoming the home of the Nabateans, Arab Bedouins. The fortress of Machaerus, was most likely where John the Baptist was confined and where he was killed.

This chapter, however, focuses on only one location, Mount Nebo. Mt. Nebo is where Moses, the servant of the LORD, who had led Israel through the 40-years in the wilderness to this very spot on the verge of the promised land, went to die. From here he viewed the land Israel would inherit. Dr. Nathaniel J. Wilson wrote "The Death of Moses" (*Ultimate Leadership: The Defining Moment*, Sacramento, CA, 2003). It appears here with his permission.

Death of Moses by Dr. Nathaniel Wilson

The two most poignant moments in history are Calvary and the death of Moses. When he dies, Moses is not spoken of as either a master of the people or as a servant of the people. Moses belongs to God and God alone. He is "the servant of the Lord." Moses is the most complete leader in history. Other leaders did some things which Moses did. But the versatility of Moses as a single leader is without parallel. His ability to learn, to discern the leadership forms which matched the people, and to locate people in their movement forward while, at the same time, preventing them from self-destructing, stands in stark contrast to all others. Outside of Christ, there is no one like Moses. He is the most complete leader in history.

Nevertheless, after 40 years of wilderness leadership, he cannot go into the Promise Land. There is no scene in the Old Testament more touching than the final days of Moses. God and Moses . . . old partners and friends . . . not unlike a Father with a grown son who possess a depth of mutual love and intimacy beyond words. Moses is God's man, God's leader. Moses asks if he can enter the Promise Land. God beckons Moses to come with Him and they slowly walk together from the plains to near the top of Nebo. Here Moses is bid to view the present kingdoms of this world (Canaan) and the glory of them. Here they stand, God and his man at an historic occasion with universal and eternal implications. Together in an intimate silence, admiring the land, the goal, the objective of four decades of leadership. With heart pounding, Moses listens in rapt attention as God, taking His time, points first right, then left, thoroughly outlining for Moses where each of the tribes will reside.

> *"And the Lord showed him all the land of Gilead, unto Dan, And all Naphtali, and the land of Ephraim and Manasseh, and all the land of Judah, unto the utmost sea, And the south, and the plain of the valley of Jericho, the city of palm trees, unto Zoar. And the Lord said unto him, This is the land…."* (Deut.34:1-4).

What a grand visual tour . . . with God as the tour guide, pointing here and then there, singling out points of interest, borders, characteristics of the land, and other incidentals. Moses is enraptured by the sheer grandeur of it all.

When He is finished, God perhaps asks, "My dear Moses, do you have any further questions?"

"No, Master," replies Moses with excitement. "When can we go in?"

"Well, Moses, the people you have led will be going in shortly. But you are not going in," God replies.

"You mean after forty years of faithful leadership, after enduring rebellions, insurrections, famines, war, and the stress of thousands of leadership decisions and acts, I'm not going to be allowed to go in!?" asks Moses, with an unbelieving and incredulous look on his face.

"That's right, Moses," responds God, calmly but firmly.

"But God . . ." Moses begins.

"That's it, Moses. No. You are not going in, period. End of discussion," God strongly responds.

What sadness! What disappointment! Consider it. A whole life spent fulfilling God's mission—and fulfilling it successfully. A man who has, through herculean efforts and with sagacity never before or after seen in human history, will be left alone, unrewarded, on the very precipice of the fulfillment. Here they are, at the river. They WILL go in. But now, the one responsible for it all is going to be left out, outside, alone, unfound, unvisited. Left in a strange and foreign land among a strange and foreign people. How can Moses even attempt to understand this hard and austere God to whom he is servant?

God's actions are strange. Moses watches. Quietly, and with a warm half-smile, God takes the hand of Moses and, with a firm grip, moves resolutely up the short distance to the top of the mountain. Slowly God turns and moves close to Moses. There, alone, steely-eyed and never flinching, God looks Moses in the eye as his life begins to seep from him.

Moses knows God can save him . . . and waits. But God never relents, never shows emotion, but holds his stoic and unrelenting gaze. Moses waits. God never blinks. No tears. No compromise. The eyes of Moses look pleadingly into the face of God but to no avail. Moses dies . . . dies never knowing how deeply God feels toward him, never knowing that the heart of divinity breaks. Finally, the last breath leaves his body. He is gone, his journey ending on this lonely, barren, windswept mount, never to be found again.

Ah, but what is that we hear? A moan, sounding like some divine lament! We look and listen as an unspeakably deep, heaving, divine sob escapes! Oh, perhaps we don't belong here! We are in a poignant moment and place. Tell no man, but ***God weeps!*** Wait! Now, with divine arms of affection, God slowly bends and tenderly lifts the slack body of his faithful servant, lifts him as one would lift a precious newborn. With emotion of some infinite proportion, He carries him, mumbling softly and lovingly to the slack corpse. There, God takes his dear servant to a secret and special burial place. There, in the solitude of the long fingers of the deepening shadows of evening, He gently lowers the body of his friend, Moses. God, with infinite tenderness, lays him to rest. The Bible then says a strange thing:

> *"And there arose not a prophet since in Israel like unto Moses, whom the Lord knew face to face"* (Deut. 34:10).

Knew face to face? What does this mean? How *did* Moses die? God, looking into the now tranquil face of his beloved servant quietly and carefully kneels beside him. Then, slowly bending forward, He looks into the now composed face of His beloved servant and with a tearful tenderness only possible to divinity, God comes close and closer . . . and ever so gently . . . bows and kisses him. Face to face. Kissed by God! A kiss of love! A kiss of death! A kiss good -bye! But a kiss from God! Isn't that a greater reward than . . . yes, that's right . . . than anything.

And some thought there was then a moaning of the wind and a splash of rain. Others thought it was like a divine groan and thought maybe they heard the small splashes of falling tears, and heard a voice, with deep and utter pain, brokenly say, "O, my Moses! O, my precious, precious, faithful, loved, Moses!" Then, gently closing the unseeing eyes, almost apologetically, He said, "Soon I will awaken you. And you shall join another, and converse with Him in the land of promise. He will also stand on a wilderness mount looking into the land . . . but nothing shall be able to stop Him from leading my people there" (Eph. 4:8-10, Ps. 2:7-9, 12).

Moses, the greatest leader . . . is . . . gone.

42

Historical Ages and Periods in the Middle East

Bronze Age – c. 3300 B.C. – c. 1200 B.C.

The Bronze Age is named for the widespread use of bronze which was made from mined and smelted tin and was added to hot copper to make bronze alloy. This was a tremendous advancement in technology making possible the mass production of weapons, jewelry, cooking and eating utensils. The Bronze Age in the Bible Lands (Near East or Levant) can be divided into three periods, Early, Middle and Late. Each of the main three periods is also divided into shorter periods which are convenient for dating various findings in archeological layers. In the right-hand column are the dates of the births of Bible figures or other significant events as estimated by the Reese Chronological Bible. Genesis 4:22 records Tubalcain, the son of Lamech as "an instructor of every worker in brass and iron." This would have been earlier than the Early Bronze Age and much earlier than the Iron Age, signifying that the art of making iron (if the iron mentioned here was of the same materials as what appeared later) was lost during the flood and took many years to rediscover. These figures are rough and there are exceptions such as the biblical account and others. I.e., small iron artifacts dated to 3200 B.C. were found in burials in Lower Egypt.

Early Bronze Age (EBA) – 3300-2100 B.C.

3300-3000: EBA I

3288 – Methuselah

3000-2700: EBA II

2919 – Noah

2700-2200: EBA III

2319 – The Flood

2200-2100: EBA IV

2144 – Tower of Babel

Middle Bronze Age (MBA) – 2100-1550 B.C.

2100-2000: MBA I

2097 – Terah

2000-1750: MBA II A

1967 – Abraham, 1807 – Jacob

1750-1650: MBA II B

Jacob into Egypt – 1677

1650-1550: MBA II C

March 6, 1543 – Moses

Late Bronze Age (LBA) – 1550-1200 B.C.

1550-1400: LBA I

April 15, 1462 – First Passover

1400-1300: LBA II A

Joshua and the Judges

1300-1177: LBA II B (Collapse of Civilization)

The Judges

The Collapse of Civilization is also called the Collapse of the Bronze Age. Archaeologists suggest a perfect storm of events combined to cause this collapse, including drought, famine, earthquakes, sociopolitical unrest, and invasion by the Sea Peoples. This collapse of culture resulted in a worldwide shortage of tin, which led to a scarcity of bronze. Eric Cline quotes Carol

Bell as saying, "the strategic importance of tin in the Late Bronze Age was probably not far different from that of crude oil today."[6]

Iron Age 1177-539 B.C.

The Iron Age lasted in the Ancient Middle East from roughly 1177-539 B.C. Even though the promised land contained iron ore (Deut 8:9), by the days of Samuel and Saul there were no iron workers in Israel. The trade was controlled by the Philistines.

David caused Israel to prosper in the iron business with some even suggesting that he had discovered the Philistines' secrets during the time he spent with them. He accumulated valuable material for the building of the temple, including "Of the gold, the silver, and the brass, and the iron, there is no number" (1 Chron 22:16).

Even in the days of the kings, iron was so valuable that when one of the sons of the prophets lost his axe head in the waters of the Jordan, he told Elisha who caused the iron to float to the surface and be recovered (2 Kings 6:5-7). Iron, when heated with carbon made steel, which was much harder than either iron or bronze and could hold an edge much longer. The iron age in the Ancient Middle East is divided into IA1 – 1200-1000 B.C. and IA2 1000-550 B.C.

---

[6] Cline, Eric H., *1177 B.C. THE YEAR CIVILIZATION COLLAPSED*, Princeton University Press: Princeton, NJ, 2021, p. xvii.

Historical Periods

Following the Iron Age, the history of the Levant is divided into various "Historical Periods" based on the dominant power in the region. They are generally considered as follows:

Babylonian and Persian Periods.........................586 B.C. – 332 B.C.
Hellenistic (Greek) Period ....332 B.C.– 37 B.C.
Hasmonean Dynasty...140 B.C. – 37 B.C.
Roman Period..37 B.C. – 324 A.D.
Byzantine Period ....324 A.D. – 638 A.D.
Early Arab Period
Umayyad...661 A.D. – 750 A.D.
Abbasid..750 A.D.– 1099 A.D.
Ayyubid...1171 A.D. – 1260 A.D.
Crusader Period...1099 A.D. – 1291 A.D.
Late Arab Period (Fatimid and Mamluk)...1291 A.D. – 1516 A.D.
Ottoman Period...1516 A.D.– 1917 A.D.
Modern Period... 1917 A.D. to Present

Bible Land Journey Map

1. Lod and Ono
2. Joppa
3. Caesarea by the Sea
4. Roman Aqueduct
5. Mt. Carmel
6. Tel Megiddo
7. Gidon Springs
8. Sea of Galilee
9. Capernaum
10. Chorazin
11. Hazor
12. Dan
13. Caesarea Philippi
14. Mt. Hermon
15. Bethshean
16. Jordan Valley
17. Jericho
18. Masada
19. Engedi
20. Qumran
21. Dead Sea
22. Jericho Road
23. Shiloh
24. Jerusalem
25. Valley of Elah
26. Azekah
27. Beersheba
28. Mount Nebo

NOTE: The locations are not in exact locations on the map or to scale for distance.

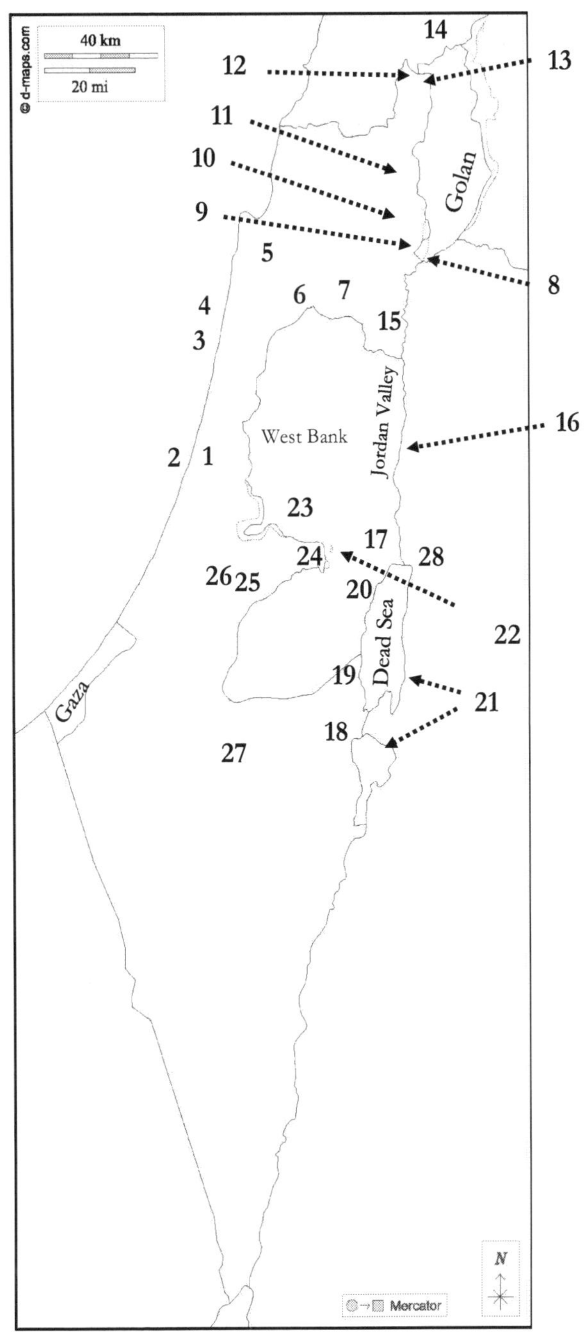

© d-maps.com
40 km
20 mi
14
12
13
11
10
Golan
9
5
8
4
6
7
15
3
Jordan Valley
16
West Bank
2
1
23
17
28
24
26
25
20
Dead Sea
22
19
21
Gaza
18
27
N
Mercator

Index of Scriptures

Index of Scriptures, cont.

Index of Scriptures

Index of Scriptures, cont.

Index

Made in the USA
Columbia, SC
31 July 2023